NATIONAL GEOGRAPHIC KiDS

weird but true!

know-it-all

U.S. Presidents

MOUNT RUSHMORE, IN SOUTH DAKOTA, U.S.A., FEATURES THE FACES OF PRESIDENTS GEORGE WASHINGTON, THOMAS JEFFERSON, THEODORE ROOSEVELT, AND ABRAHAM LINCOLN

NATIONAL GEOGRAPHIC KiDS

weird but true!

know-it-all

U.S. Presidents

BRIANNA DUMONT

ILLUSTRATED BY ADRIAN LUBBERS

NATIONAL GEOGRAPHIC
WASHINGTON, D.C.

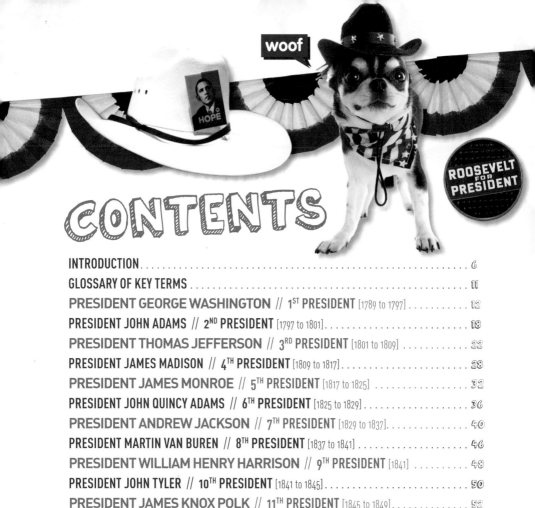

woof

CONTENTS

JOB DESCRIPTION NOT INCLUDED

The framers of the Constitution were fed up with kings. They didn't want to create a new government with too much power, but they also knew a stronger government could help get things done. The question was how to check and balance that power.

History didn't help. There was a lack of examples of effective republics from around the world to help them decide how much and what kind of power the leader of their new country should have. Since there was no precedent to follow, the first president, George Washington, realized that all of his decisions would define what it means to be the president. Ever since, different presidents have shaped the presidency in their own way, so it can be said that the job description is still evolving even today.

BY THE NUMBERS

Did you know the White House has a dentist, a florist shop, and a chocolate shop? While the most famous house in the country is constantly updating with each new president, here are some fast facts:

ADDRESS	1600 PENNSYLVANIA AVE.		STAIRCASES	8
SIZE	55,000 SQUARE FEET (5,110 SQ M)		ELEVATORS	3
GALLONS OF PAINT TO KEEP IT WHITE	570 (2,158 L)		HIDDEN MEZZANINE LEVELS	2
FLOORS	6		BOMB SHELTERS	1
WINDOWS	147		SECRET TUNNELS	0 THAT WE KNOW OF!
ROOMS	132			
FIREPLACES	28			

RENOVATION NATION

The White House is pretty iconic, but it does get updates every now and then. Incoming presidents even get to pick out personal touches for the Oval Office, including rugs, paint color, curtains, statues, and pictures. The only thing about the Oval Office that doesn't change is the shape!

Here's a history of some of the more necessary updates to the White House:

1801 Indoor bathroom (JEFFERSON)

1831 Running water (JACKSON)

1837 Central heat (VAN BUREN)

1848 Gas lighting (POLK)

1879 Telephone (HAYES)

1882 Elevators (ARTHUR)

1891 Electric lights (HARRISON)

1922 Radio (HARDING)

1933 Heated swimming pool (FDR)

1978 Computers (CARTER)

GEORGE WASHINGTON IS THE ONLY PRESIDENT NOT TO LIVE IN THE WHITE HOUSE!

RESIDENCE PESTILENCE

Despite what you've been told, Washington, D.C., was not built on a swamp. It was built on watery tidal lands by the Potomac River. The land was a mixture of forests and waterways. All that standing water made a perfect breeding ground for mosquitoes. Those bloodsucking nuisances not only itched, they carried death and disease. One doctor even tried to get the capital to put a huge mosquito net around the whole city! (He failed.) Now, levees help hold back the floodwaters, but even today, a good rain will flood the sidewalks by the Jefferson Memorial.

POWERS OF THE PRESIDENT

WHAT CAN THE PRESIDENT DO?

>> Grant pardons to federal offenders
>> Make treaties (that have to be approved by the Senate)
>> Appoint judges and ambassadors (who have to be approved by the Senate)
>> Call Congress into session during "extraordinary occasions"
>> Enforce laws
>> Veto bills
>> Support legislation
>> Issue executive orders

"VETO" MEANS "I FORBID" IN LATIN.

POWERS OF CONGRESS

IN RETURN, CONGRESS HAS THE POWER TO "CHECK," OR LIMIT, THE PRESIDENT'S POWER. IT CAN:

>> Override the president's vetoes with a two-thirds majority
>> Reject his appointments
>> Reject his treaties
>> Declare war
>> Impeach the president

THREE BRANCHES OF GOVERNMENT

LEGISLATIVE (MAKES LAWS)	EXECUTIVE (CARRIES OUT LAWS)	JUDICIAL (EVALUATES LAWS)
CONGRESS	PRESIDENT	SUPREME COURT
SENATE	VICE PRESIDENT	FEDERAL COURTS
HOUSE OF REPRESENTATIVES	CABINET	

POWERS OF THE SUPREME COURT

The Supreme Court can declare acts from the president and Congress "unconstitutional," but that's not stated in the Constitution. It's thanks to a court ruling in 1803. (Check out the Thomas Jefferson chapter!)

GETTING ELECTED

The road to the White House doesn't have a map—figuratively speaking at least! Anybody who's a natural born citizen, is over 35 years of age, and is a resident for at least 14 years can become president. Presidents have come from rags and riches. But here's how the process works on election day.

The framers of the Constitution weren't too jazzed about the idea of the people directly electing their leader. That seemed a little risky. So when people go to the polls today, they aren't voting for president. Not technically. They're voting for electors who are pledged to vote for a specific candidate. This process is called the electoral college, and the electors are the ones who cast a vote for president in December. Their votes are based on who their state's citizens voted for in November.

Sometimes, more people vote for a candidate, which is called the popular vote, but that candidate still doesn't win because he or she didn't get enough electoral votes. This has happened five times!

Each state gets as many electors as they have representatives and senators in Congress. Each state always gets two senators, and the number of representatives is based on its population. There's a total of 538 electors (the District of Columbia gets three electors, despite having no votes in Congress), and the candidate who reaches 270 electoral votes wins the White House!

PICKING UP THE TAB

PERSONAL EXPENSES ARE NOT INCLUDED IN THE PRESIDENT'S JOB DESCRIPTION. IF YOU WERE PRESIDENT, YOU WOULD HAVE TO PAY FOR THINGS LIKE TOOTHPASTE AND MOUTHWASH YOURSELF!

MORE **AMENDMENTS** HAVE BEEN PROPOSED TO REFORM OR KILL THE **ELECTORAL COLLEGE** THAN ANY OTHER SUBJECT.

BURNING DOWN THE WHITE HOUSE

The President's House, as it was originally called, earned the nickname "White House" from the white paint first applied to it in 1798 to protect the stone from the effects of weather. During the War of 1812, the British made it all the way to D.C., and in 1814 they set the White House on fire! (Before she fled, First Lady Dolley Madison stopped to save a portrait of George Washington from the inferno!) While the wood was burned to a crisp, the still-standing sandstone bricks were only scorched, so the White House got a new coat of white paint.

CAST OF CHARACTERS

It takes a lot of people to keep the White House running. The 96 full-time and 250 part-time staff includes butlers, valets, carpenters, electricians, painters, chefs, maids, and florists!

GHOSTS

A few ghosts have been said to roam the hallowed hallways as well. People have reported seeing Abigail Adams, Andrew Jackson, and Abraham Lincoln, who is said to have once scared a naked Winston Churchill!

JAMES MONROE HAD TO **WAIT** UNTIL SEPTEMBER 1817 TO MOVE INTO THE **WHITE HOUSE** SINCE IT WAS STILL BEING RENOVATED AFTER THE **BRITISH SCORCHING!**

WHITE HOUSE PASTRY CHEF

IF WE ARE GOING TO TALK ABOUT THE OFFICE OF THE PRESIDENT, WE'RE GOING TO NEED TO KNOW SOME BIG WORDS. HERE ARE SOME IMPORTANT TERMS YOU'LL FIND IN THE COMING PAGES.

ANNEXATION To formally declare a piece of land for a different country, without a treaty or money from a sale

ACQUIT To set free from a criminal charge

BILL A proposed law given to Congress for debate

CHECKS AND BALANCES A system to ensure that no one branch of government becomes too powerful

CONSTITUTION A document that defines the beliefs and laws of a country

CONTINENTAL CONGRESS The assembly of delegates from the 13 colonies who met before, during, and in the years immediately following the Revolutionary War for independence from Britain

DRAFT A requirement of military service for young men

ELECTORAL COLLEGE The process by which the country elects its president

EXECUTIVE BRANCH The president is the head of the executive branch and the country. He or she is responsible for signing and enforcing laws passed by Congress.

EXECUTIVE ORDER The implied power of the president (not in the Constitution) to give an order with the legal status of a law

IMPEACH To charge the president with a crime

INAUGURATION The swearing in of a new president who promises to do his or her best for the country, based on the U.S. Constitution

INCOME TAX A yearly charge based on a person's salary

INFLATION An increase in the price of things, such as goods or services

JUDICIAL BRANCH The court system in the U.S., with the Supreme Court at the top. Supreme Court justices are judges who decide if the laws passed by Congress or executive orders signed by the president are constitutional and legal. The Supreme Court also hears cases whose rulings in lower courts have been challenged.

LEGISLATIVE BRANCH The law-creation system in the U.S., in which members are voted in by the people. Congress writes and revises bills to send to the president to sign into laws. If the president vetoes one, they can override the veto with a two-thirds majority and make it into a law.

PARDON To officially forgive someone for a crime

PENSION An amount of money paid to a person once they retire or at the end of their career

POCKET VETO A tactic used to stop a bill from becoming a law by ignoring the bill until it's too late to sign it or formally veto it

TARIFF A type of tax on goods going in and out of a country

TREATY A formal agreement between nations

TRUST A large business, or multiple businesses put together, that controls the prices of its products and reduces competition

VETO A presidential power used to stop a bill from becoming a law

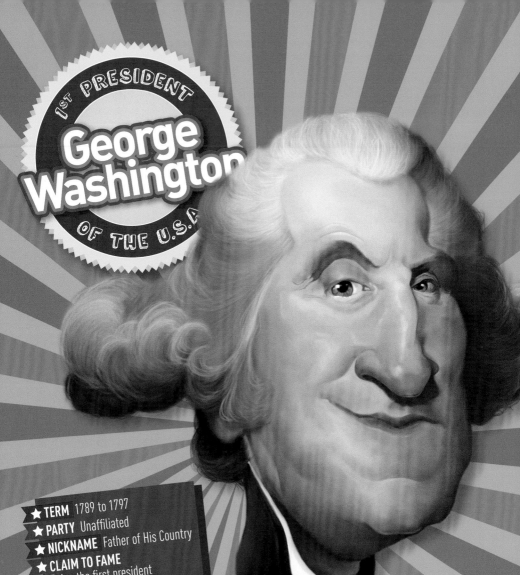

1ST PRESIDENT
George Washington
OF THE U.S.A.

★ **TERM** 1789 to 1797
★ **PARTY** Unaffiliated
★ **NICKNAME** Father of His Country
★ **CLAIM TO FAME**
Being the first president
★ **BORN** Pope's Creek, Virginia
★ **FIRST LADY** Martha Washington
(married 1759 to 1799)

"I walk on untrodden ground ...
There is scarcely any part of my
conduct which may not hereafter
be drawn into precedent."

G Washington

WHY HE'S WEIRD While general of the Continental Army, Washington refused a salary and asked only to be compensated for his expenses. Then he spent $160,074—millions in ▶▶▶

George Washington was not born with a silver spoon, but he didn't exactly come from humble beginnings. His father was a plantation owner in 18th-century Virginia and he provided a comfortable life for his wife and nine children. George helped manage the farm, but he could also hang with the aristocrats (wealthy noblemen) and wear silk stockings. He had his eye on greatness from an early age, longing to move above his family's station. And he succeeded. By the end of his life, Washington helped create the longest-lasting republic the world has ever seen—the United States of America.

MONUMENTAL MISTAKES

Born into a second marriage, young Washington went through life trying to prove himself. He didn't get the same formal education that his older half brothers received, since his father passed away when he was 11, leaving the family with less money to spare and in need of more help around the plantation. But he was naturally smart and curious, and loved a good adventure. He spent his teens surveying (mapping out) unexplored wilderness and secured the position of county surveyor by age 17. But war came calling, and Washington was all too eager to answer.

In the years leading up to 1753, Britain (and the American colonies) was arguing with its eternal enemy, France, over territory in North America. In one of his first missions as the leader of a Virginia militia company, Washington and his men launched a surprise attack in disputed territory and killed 10 Frenchmen, including the messenger, who was just delivering news to the British. His troops retreated to a nearby fort, which was eventually surrounded by the French, and he was forced to surrender the battle. The French and Indian War—part of the larger Seven Years' War—was soon ignited, but a humiliated Washington resigned his position. He would not be off the battlefield for long. He later served as an aide to an important British general during the war, gaining valuable experience.

gulp!

DOWN WITH THE CROWN

After the French and Indian War, Britain kept control of most of North America. Washington's side had won!

today's dollars!—on personal expenses, headquarters costs, and travel.

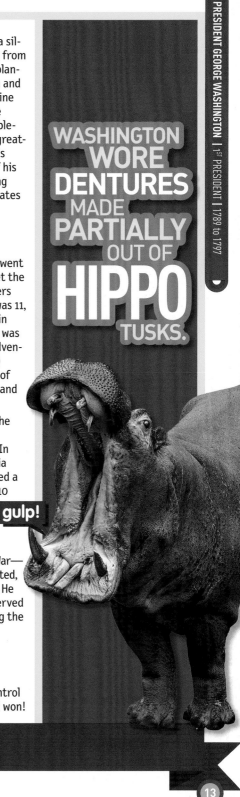

WASHINGTON **WORE DENTURES** MADE **PARTIALLY** OUT OF **HIPPO** TUSKS.

But there was new tension growing. American colonists were getting pretty sick of answering to Parliament (the British government in London). The war with the French had rendered the British broke, and Parliament decided to increase the taxes in the colonies to make up the difference. Many colonists—both the powerful and powerless—protested. After all, the colonists couldn't even elect someone to represent them in Parliament. Eventually there was also debate over the very idea of a monarch—a king or queen—being born into such a powerful position.

After years of protests, discussions, and conflicts, most people were ready for independence, and Washington agreed that the British had to go. But first, the colonists needed a leader.

DRESSED TO IMPRESS

George Washington wanted to remind people that he was battle-tested, and that he looked good in a uniform. After a year of service in the Continental Congress, in 1775 he showed up in his old militia uniform and sat quietly waiting for everyone to notice.

Since he was the only one with any real military experience and had a tremendous reputation, Congress unanimously voted him their commander in chief of the Continental Army. He responded humbly, "I do not think myself equal to the command." Which might have been true. His only experiences in war included losing, retreating, and surrendering, but by this point that was water under the bridge.

His first command was to himself: Read some books and study up on how to be a general.

PRIMING FOR THE PRESIDENCY

The Revolutionary War lasted six years and had a lot of ups and downs for Washington. He lost more battles than he won, and fighting defensively was still his go-to tactic. But he was a good leader: He kept the spirits of his troops high through grueling weather and gut-wrenching defeats. In the end, by inspiring them to greatness, he himself became great. Whether he was wrangling funds and supplies from a reluctant Congress or forming a secret spy ring, Washington proved he was the best man for the job. And with the help of officers who were better at tactics, he led his men against the most powerful military in the Western world—and won.

FIRST THINGS FIRST

The Revolutionary War was over, but now came the hard part: figuring out the best way to govern the land. At first, Washington retired to his plantation, happy to be home. But the Articles of Confederation (the document that outlined the laws of the land before the U.S. Constitution was written), created 13 separate states without a strong central government. They'd done this on purpose, as a reaction to what they considered British tyranny, or abuse of power. Not much got done since the states couldn't agree on economic or foreign policies. Washington agreed to be president of the Constitutional Convention, which was supposed to change the Articles of Confederation, but ended up creating a new foundation for the country instead.

Using a framework provided by James Madison, men from each state (except Rhode Island, which didn't send any delegates) worked together to write a new constitution that increased federal (national) power. From there, Washington was only one step away from being unanimously voted in as the first president of the United States!

PRACTICAL PRECEDENTS

Because everyone trusted Washington, they left the president's job description rather murky. It would be up to him to figure out everything from shaping foreign policy to throwing dinner parties. He knew the eyes of the nation were upon him, so he acted carefully. He wouldn't even veto a bill until 1792—three years after becoming president!

THOMAS VERSUS ALEXANDER

Washington became successful during the war by surrounding himself with people whose expertise made him a stronger leader. He wanted his government to have a similar setup for success.

VICES OF THE PRESIDENT

SOME OF THE PRECEDENTS WASHINGTON SET WERE DUE TO HIS LEGENDARY TEMPER. AFTER GETTING INTO REPEATED ARGUMENTS WITH HIS VICE PRESIDENT, JOHN ADAMS, WASHINGTON STOPPED INVITING ADAMS TO MEETINGS, OR ASKING HIS ADVICE. THIS SET THE STAGE FOR VICE PRESIDENTS NOT BEING AS INVOLVED IN FORMAL GOVERNMENT BUSINESS.

FANCY FROLICKING

It's no surprise that people wanted to hang out with Washington. He was a hero! But small talk wasn't his favorite. Alexander Hamilton suggested weekly receptions on Tuesday afternoons for men only. At 3 p.m., Washington would greet the men wearing black velvet and yellow gloves (and his sword, of course). Everyone would stand in a circle and bow, because Washington didn't approve of handshaking. Washington addressed each man once, and a few words would be exchanged. At 4 p.m. on the dot, it was over. Apparently nobody enjoyed it.

VS.

JEFFERSON

HAMILTON

He knew he didn't know everything, so he created the first presidential Cabinet (a body of advisers). Instead of storing plates and bowls, Washington's Cabinet stored his most trusted confidants whom he called on for advice.

Unfortunately, two of his most trusted advisers were also enemies. Thomas Jefferson and Alexander Hamilton fought about everything. As president, Washington had to take sides, and he often sided with Hamilton. Jefferson eventually quit in protest. This started another precedent—political parties.

TAKING CARE OF BUSINESS

A big part of the beef between Hamilton and Jefferson was about money. Hamilton was a Federalist and wanted a big bank run by businessmen, and he wanted to encourage industry and trade. Jefferson was a Democratic-Republican and wanted farmers to rule America. He worried that a big bank would control the government and people.

Hamilton's plan also included a tax hike on whiskey. Farmers across the United States did not like the sound of that. They just went to war to end unfair taxation!

Many rural residents in Pennsylvania decided they'd protest, just like they did against Parliament and King George. President George was having none of that. When he asked his Cabinet for advice, they couldn't agree, so Washington decided for himself.

He saddled up once more and led 13,000 troops into Pennsylvania. Upon hearing they were coming, the protesters gave up and went home before Washington even arrived. There was no need for battle, and as a result, Washington's show of power strengthened the powers of the presidency to boot.

EXECUTIVE EXHAUSTION

The last tradition Washington set wasn't intentional. After two terms, Washington just wanted peace and quiet at his home in Mount Vernon, so he declined a third term. No other president has served longer than two terms except Franklin D. Roosevelt in the 1940s! Although he'd given up power, Washington left happier than a clam.

Many of the precedents Washington created are still in place today, and his legacy is everywhere. He has a state, cities, monuments, and buildings

LONG LIVE MR. PRESIDENT

WASHINGTON HAD JUST SPENT SIX YEARS RIDDING THE LAND OF ONE MONARCH. HE WASN'T ABOUT TO BECOME ONE HIMSELF. SOME PEOPLE, ACCUSTOMED TO ANSWERING TO A KING, DIDN'T UNDERSTAND. DURING HIS INAUGURATION, THEY SANG A VERSION OF "GOD SAVE THE KING," AND "LONG LIVE GEORGE WASHINGTON," AND PUT LAUREL WREATHS ON HIS HEAD. INSTEAD OF BEDECKING HIMSELF IN JEWELS AND A CROWN, WASHINGTON WORE A SIMPLE BROWN SUIT, WHICH STARTED ANOTHER PRECEDENT: PRESIDENTS WEARING REGULAR-PEOPLE CLOTHING.

bearing his name. In 1789 when Washington was sworn in, the presidency was not the respected position it is today. No one knew what to expect, and many were suspicious of the amount of power a president could wield. Washington made the presidency something to be respected.

ROOM WITH A VIEW

Another perk of being the first president was having influence in picking a site for the new capital. After much discussion, it was decided that the capital would be on the Potomac River. Washington's opinion had a lot of sway, and he wanted it near his Mount Vernon estate on the Potomac. The states of Maryland and Virginia both gave up some land to create a perfect little pocket in between. The commissioners in charge of setting up the new city named it in the president's honor, and Washington, D.C., was born.

MOUNT VERNON, GEORGE WASHINGTON'S HOME IN VIRGINIA

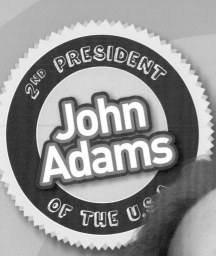

2ND PRESIDENT John Adams OF THE U.S.A.

- ★ **TERM** 1797 to 1801
- ★ **PARTY** Federalist
- ★ **NICKNAME** His Rotundity
- ★ **CLAIM TO FAME** XYZ Affair
- ★ **BORN** Braintree, Massachusetts
- ★ **FIRST LADY** Abigail Adams (married 1764 to 1818)

"Facts are stubborn things."

John Adams

I ♥ ABBY

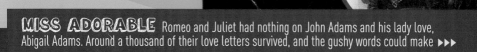

MISS ADORABLE Romeo and Juliet had nothing on John Adams and his lady love, Abigail Adams. Around a thousand of their love letters survived, and the gushy words could make ▶▶▶

Sandwiched between Washington and Jefferson, John Adams's legacy tends to get overshadowed. He shaped America from the very beginning, and the poor guy doesn't even have a monument on the National Mall (though one has been long discussed)! But Adams accomplished more even before he became president than some presidents do during their term. He was critical in Massachusetts politics, played an important role at the Continental Congress, nominated Washington for general, recommended Jefferson to draft the Declaration of Independence, and wrote miles and miles of papers about the best way to govern the new states!

UNPOPULARITY CONTEST

John Adams did not have a powerful physical presence like Washington, but he was smart and wily, and he used both to excel in life. In school, he loved to play hooky and go fishing, but still aced all his classes. As a high-powered lawyer (before his presidency), he tended to do unpopular things, like defend

JOHN ADAMS WAS 90 WHEN HE DIED— THE LONGEST LIVING PRESIDENT UNTIL RONALD REAGAN—178 YEARS LATER!

the redcoats (British soldiers) who killed five protesters in 1770 in the Boston Massacre. He succeeded at keeping them alive, when everyone else was out for redcoat blood.

Washington and Adams did have one thing in common: They were both a bit vain. At one point when he was in Paris, Adams bragged in his diary about how much the French admired him. Then he "accidentally" sent his diary to Congress along with an official report. Congress responded by reading it aloud to everyone.

FIERY FRENEMIES

John Adams called the vice presidency "the most insignificant office ... ever." He should know, since he was the first. George Washington

Cupid roll his eyes: "I presume I have good right to draw upon you for the kisses, as I have given two or three million at least ..."

didn't want his advice so Adams didn't have much to do. But then, Washington retired after two terms, igniting the first real election. It was a doozy.

Thomas Jefferson and John Adams ran against each other, and their supporters didn't pull any punches. The campaign was full of dirty tricks and name-calling, although it was not as bad as when the two faced off again in 1800! When it was all said and done, Adams barely squeaked out the win.

At that time, the person in second place became vice president. For Adams, that meant Thomas Jefferson was now his right-hand man. They used to be friends, but then politics got in the way. Now they were just enemies.

ALPHABET SOUP

Once in office, Adams found revolutionary France—which was in the throes of a violent, murderous revolution itself—to be a nuisance. They had killed their king and were at war with Britain. In 1794, Britain and the United States signed the Jay Treaty to diplomatically resolve outstanding issues and tensions stemming from the Revolution. The French were outraged. They felt the treaty betrayed the traditional U.S.-France friendship and violated an older treaty that the U.S. had with France. In response, the French government ordered that American merchant (trade) ships could be seized and searched.

Years later, when Adams was president, he sent diplomats (people who represent the U.S. abroad) to France to work things out without resorting to war, but things in France were a bit chaotic at the time, in the aftermath of their own revolution and war with their hated rival, Britain. The French prime minister demanded a hefty bribe to even meet American diplomats. The diplomats refused.

Adams didn't want to give in to the French, but members of the opposition Democratic-Republican Party demanded that the president hand over the reports that the American diplomats had sent to him. Adams promptly handed them over, but replaced the French names with X, Y, and Z.

PEACEMAKER

The XYZ Affair made Adams an instant hit. Suddenly, everyone loved him for refusing to give in to the French, and Congress gave him permission and money for defense measures. Adams created the Navy and the Marines, and he asked George Washington to lead an army. By this time the aging general was no spring chicken, but that didn't matter. Everyone still trusted him.

Washington agreed, but then he died. Luckily for the nation, war against France was never declared. Adams said his greatest accomplishment was keeping the peace when it was needed the most.

WHY HE'S WEIRD!

JOHN ADAMS AND THOMAS JEFFERSON—ON-AGAIN, OFF-AGAIN PALS—BOTH DIED ON THE FIFTIETH ANNIVERSARY OF THE SIGNING OF THE DECLARATION OF INDEPENDENCE, THE FOURTH OF JULY. WITHOUT KNOWING JEFFERSON HAD DIED THAT MORNING, ADAMS'S LAST WORDS WERE REPORTEDLY, "THOMAS JEFFERSON SURVIVES."

FRENCH FRIGHT

Adams didn't want anything or anyone (like the French) to topple the new country, so he tried his best to protect it. Unfortunately, he defied the Constitution that he helped champion.

He signed the Alien and Sedition Acts, which could deport anyone who wasn't a citizen and was believed to be dangerous. Becoming a citizen went from a five-year to a 14-year process. Even scarier, no one could badmouth the government or they'd face jail. In other words, freedom of speech went out the window.

MIDNIGHT COURT

Even though Adams didn't deport anyone, 10 men were convicted under the Sedition Act. In the next election, Jefferson used the unpopularity of the Alien and Sedition Acts to help him win against Adams.

sacrebleu!

Adams was pretty bitter, so he left Jefferson with a parting present. During his last day in office—all the way up to midnight—he filled vacant and newly created judicial offices with men he wanted. Then he left town at four in the morning to avoid Jefferson's inauguration. His judicial appointments would annoy Jefferson for the next eight years, and they laid the groundwork for the judicial branch.

3RD PRESIDENT
Thomas Jefferson
OF THE U.S.A.

- ★ **TERM** 1801 to 1809
- ★ **PARTY** Democratic-Republican
- ★ **NICKNAME** Sage of Monticello
- ★ **CLAIM TO FAME** Louisiana Purchase
- ★ **BORN** Shadwell Plantation, Virginia
- ★ **SPOUSE** Martha Jefferson (married 1772 to 1782; died at age 33, 20 years before Jefferson won the presidency)

"The tree of liberty must be refreshed from time to time with the blood of patriots and tyrants."

Th Jefferson

ONE LORD A-LEAPING While in Paris, Jefferson hoped to impress his lady companion by jumping over a low fence. Instead of looking lordly while leaping in his breeches and ▶▶▶

Having lived through the Revolutionary War to break free from the British crown, Thomas Jefferson didn't exactly trust people in positions of power. If he had his way, everyone in America would be farmers, the federal government would be weak, and there'd be an uprising every few years just to spice things up. He thought each state should govern as it saw fit, with little interference on a national level. That's why it's pretty funny that during his eight years as president, he governed in a manner that was, in many ways, just the opposite.

PUSHING FOR PENNIES

Before entering the White House, Jefferson had quite an impressive resume. He was a Founding Father, the author of the Declaration of Independence, ambassador to France, secretary of state, and vice president to John Adams. But that's not all he accomplished. For starters, he overhauled the entire monetary system of the young nation before becoming president.

After the American Revolution, each colony had its own way of counting coins and exchange rates, and none of those systems added up the same way. Jefferson suggested keeping it simple. He created the first decimal coinage system in the world and based it on 10s: 10 pennies made 1 dime and 10 dimes made 1 dollar; 10 10 dollars made 100 dollars. The system still stands today.

STARTING SIMPLE

Jefferson's inauguration was the first one in Washington, D.C., and he didn't want any fancy balls or wild parties to mark the occasion. Afterward, the president walked to his hotel and waited in line for dinner along with everyone else. Moving into the White House wasn't a top priority, either. Jefferson waited two weeks!

His main goals as president included undoing all the stuff that Adams did and even a few things Washington had done. Anything that smelled of monarchy had to go, too. Jefferson was so obsessed with not looking like a king, that he even received foreign ambassadors in worn-out shoes and would famously show up to meetings in a bathrobe and slippers!

AS SECRETARY OF STATE JEFFERSON ORGANIZED A CONTEST TO DESIGN THE WHITE HOUSE. HISTORIANS THINK HE THEN SECRETLY ENTERED— AND LOST!

stockings, he fell and broke his wrist. It was to be a doomed relationship anyway because the lady was already married!

READ THESE LINES OF JEFFERSON'S ORIGINAL DRAFT OF THE DECLARATION OF INDEPENDENCE AND SEE IF YOU CAN TELL WHAT HIS EDITORS, JOHN ADAMS AND BENJAMIN FRANKLIN, CHANGED. (THE ANSWER CAN BE FOUND BELOW.)

WE HOLD THESE TRUTHS TO BE SACRED AND UNDENIABLE; THAT ALL MEN ARE CREATED EQUAL & INDEPENDENT, THAT FROM THAT EQUAL CREATION THEY DERIVE RIGHTS INHERENT & INALIENABLE AMONG WHICH ARE THE PRESERVATION OF LIFE & LIBERTY & THE PURSUIT OF HAPPINESS.

WE HOLD THESE TRUTHS TO BE SELF-EVIDENT, THAT ALL MEN ARE CREATED EQUAL, THAT THEY ARE ENDOWED BY THEIR CREATOR WITH CERTAIN UNALIENABLE RIGHTS, THAT AMONG THESE ARE LIFE, LIBERTY AND THE PURSUIT OF HAPPINESS.

LEARNING TO LOSE

President Jefferson followed the Constitution down to the letter. If it didn't specifically mention something, then it wasn't legal. Since the Constitution didn't say the government could charter a national bank, then that meant NO BANK.

Now that Washington was gone, Jefferson thought he could reverse the act that created the Bank of the United States. The problem was that many people seemed to like the bank, including some people in his own party. Jefferson was quickly learning that in order to govern an entire nation, he would sometimes need to compromise his personal beliefs. After he realized how important the bank was at this early stage of the country's development, Jefferson didn't even try to get rid of it. The bank stayed. It wouldn't be the last time he modified his principles for the people.

JUDGES RULE

Even though Jefferson preached the "hands off" government philosophy, he figured he could put it into practice after he got the government back in the shape it needed to be. First he had to get rid of those last-minute judges put into place as a parting gift by John Adams.

Some of Adams's actual commission letters (giving the men their jobs) had not been delivered yet. And Jefferson said that he didn't have to deliver them! For a while, it looked like he might win. Until the Supreme Court and Chief Justice John Marshall, Jefferson's biggest judicial opponent, found a way around the president.

In the important judicial case *Marbury* v. *Madison,* Marshall ruled for the first time that it's up to the courts to decide what's constitutional and what isn't. President Jefferson couldn't do anything about it.

EVERYTHING MUST GO!

Jefferson then got an awesome opportunity. One that would literally shape the new nation. Napoleon Bonaparte, the French emperor, was a problem to a lot of people. He had one thing on

his mind, and that thing was taking over most of Europe and expanding the French Empire.

Napoleon set his sights on a grand scale, including an empire in America. But many factors, including a deadly yellow fever epidemic and a slave uprising in the French colony of Haiti, derailed Napoleon's plans. He needed money to fund another war, and he needed it fast. The decision was simple: He'd sell his land in America and focus on conquering everything east of the Atlantic instead.

Thomas Jefferson hoped to purchase New Orleans, or, at the very least, access to the valuable port there. Instead, Napoleon offered him everything from the Mississippi River to the Rocky Mountains for the low, low price of $15 million!

This put Jefferson in a pickle. Last time he checked, the Constitution didn't mention buying land. But it was such a good deal! It would automatically double the size of the U.S. That meant plenty of space to farm—the only way to be truly independent, according to Jefferson. He decided to, once again, look past his literal interpretation of the Constitution and shelled out around four cents an acre for the Louisiana Territory.

PIRATE PROBLEMS

Thomas Jefferson was determined to accomplish one thing he had set out to do at the start of his presidency: Decrease the size of the Army and Navy. Unfortunately, this idea flopped like a fish on a poop deck. Without a strong Navy, American ships were left high and dry to fend for themselves. On the northeast coast of Africa—the Barbary Coast—the leaders of those countries traditionally asked for payment in exchange for not capturing foreign ships. In 1801, the leader of Tripoli asked for more money and when he didn't get it, his pirates started seizing American ships.

Jefferson didn't want to pay, so he sent ships loaded down with cannons and gunpowder to blow the pirates out of the water. He eventually got Barbary leaders to back off, but he also realized the Navy had to stay.

SCIENCE & SCENERY

WITH THE LOUISIANA PURCHASE, AMERICA SWELLED BY 828,000 ACRES (335,080 HA). MOST OF IT WAS UNKNOWN WILDERNESS TO EUROPEANS, AND THE ONLY WAY TO SEE WHAT JEFFERSON HAD BOUGHT WAS THE OLD-FASHIONED WAY: ON FOOT. JEFFERSON COMMISSIONED THE CORPS OF DISCOVERY, HEADED BY MERIWETHER LEWIS AND WILLIAM CLARK, TO EXPLORE AND MAP OUT THE NEW TERRITORY, STUFFING THEIR KNAPSACKS WITH ANYTHING THAT LOOKED TO BE OF INTEREST. HE HOPED THEY'D FIND AN EASY WATER ROUTE ACROSS THE WHOLE LAND, BUT THE ROCKY MOUNTAINS CREATED A BIG BARRIER. FOR THREE YEARS, LEWIS, CLARK, AND THEIR AMERICAN INDIAN GUIDE, SACAGAWEA, TREKKED TO THE PACIFIC OCEAN AND BACK, LOADING THEMSELVES DOWN WITH PLANTS, ANIMALS, AND STORIES (AND SACAGAWEA DID IT ALL WITH A BABY ON HER BACK!).

REMEMBER ME

After all his accomplishments, Jefferson wanted only three things on his gravestone: author of the Declaration of Independence, and of the Statute of Virginia for Religious Freedom, and father of the University of Virginia.

SHIVER ME TRADERS

Jefferson's problems with pirates didn't end off the Barbary Coast; British and French pirates got in on the act, too. But they didn't want ransom: They wanted to "impress"—kidnap—American sailors from trade ships and recapture deserters from their own navies.

To avoid war, Jefferson pushed Congress to pass the Embargo Act, which outlawed trading with Europe. It was supposed to hit the countries right where it hurts—in their wallets—but since they were the only buyers of American goods, it backfired big time. As a result, officially, America had no buyers for their beaver pelts or tobacco or anything else. Unofficially, smuggling (illegal moving of goods out of a country) became a big business. Jefferson finally admitted defeat and changed the ban to only Britain and France. The rest of Europe was okay.

GO BIG, THEN GO HOME

In a lot of ways, Jefferson was a walking contradiction. He didn't trust strong presidents, but he actually increased presidential power more than Washington or Adams.

He also failed to reverse a bunch of policies he hated, but he did repeal the unconstitutional Alien and Sedition Acts and sprung the remaining offenders from jail.

After two terms, people still liked him, and Jefferson liked that. He decided to quit while he was ahead, just like Washington. The only thing left to do for the nation he loved was to show that it wasn't a monarchy by going home. Success!

WHY HE'S WEIRD!

JEFFERSON LOVED CHEESE, AND HE KNEW HIS ROQUEFORT FROM HIS RICOTTA! THIS FOODIE INTRODUCED FRENCH FOOD (AND FRENCH FRIES) TO AMERICA. A MASSACHUSETTS FARMER ONCE GIFTED HIM AN ALMOST 1,300-POUND (590-KG) "MAMMOTH" CHEESE IN TRIBUTE.

ALL MEN ARE NOT TREATED EQUAL

Thomas Jefferson wrote that "all men are created equal," but he owned more than 600 slaves during his life.

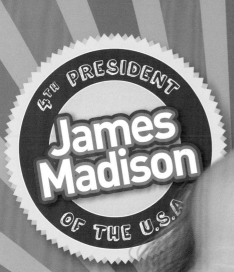

James Madison

- ★ **TERM** 1809 to 1817
- ★ **PARTY** Democratic-Republican
- ★ **NICKNAME**
  Father of the Constitution
- ★ **CLAIM TO FAME** War of 1812
- ★ **BORN** Port Conway, Virginia
- ★ **FIRST LADY** Dolley Madison
  (married 1794 to 1836)

"Knowledge will forever govern ignorance: And a people who mean to be their own Governors, must arm themselves with the power which knowledge gives."

James Madison

Bill of Rig...

WHAT'S MY LINE? Because of Madison's smooth way with words, Washington had him write his inaugural address. Then Madison wrote Congress's reply to the address, ▶▶▶

WHILE ENJOYING A SUNDAY DRIVE, MADISON AND JEFFERSON WERE ARRESTED BECAUSE CARRIAGE RIDING WAS ILLEGAL ON SUNDAYS!

James Madison may have only stood five feet four (1.6 m) and weighed 100 pounds (45 kg), but he was a giant among the Founding Fathers, mostly due to his way with words. His Virginia Plan was the blueprint for the Constitution, and it included the basis for the system of checks and balances by which the three branches of government are regulated. This means full control does not lie in any one branch's hands.

Madison also co-wrote a series of essays published in newspapers, eventually called the Federalist Papers, which aimed to reassure the skeptical new nation. People were still skittish about having a strong president and a completely new constitution, and the Federalist Papers served to ease their concerns by explaining the Constitution.

THE "RIGHT" GUY

Since the Constitution was about the way the new government should work, "We the People" wanted a few guarantees to preserve their liberty. So Madison proposed the Bill of Rights to make sure that the individual rights of the people were spelled out and protected.

The Bill of Rights is the first 10 amendments to the Constitution. Among other things, they include freedom of speech, religion, and assembly.

PRESIDENTIAL PICKLE

James Madison was Thomas Jefferson's handpicked successor. The two friends went way back to when Jefferson was the governor of Virginia, and Madison was on the state council. They had

WHY HE'S WEIRD!

MADISON LED A LONG, HEALTHY LIFE. AT THE RIPE OLD AGE OF 85, IT WAS FINALLY TIME TO GO. MADISON'S DOCTORS OFFERED TO KEEP HIM ALIVE WITH STIMULANTS SO HE COULD DIE ON THE FOURTH OF JULY LIKE FELLOW PRESIDENTS JOHN ADAMS, THOMAS JEFFERSON, AND JAMES MONROE. MADISON REFUSED. HE DIED ON JUNE 28.

AND Washington's reply to Congress's reply!

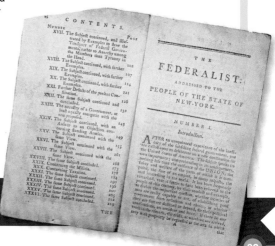

similar ideas for the nation, and a mutual respect for one another. Jefferson trusted Madison as the next leader of the United States of America. Unfortunately, by the time Madison took office, some of the policies Jefferson put into place weren't exactly working out.

America wasn't getting much respect from Europe. Jefferson's embargo had failed, and the English and French still impressed U.S. sailors by forcing them into service on their ships. Madison hoped to play Britain and France against one another, but that wasn't working either.

BACK AT IT WITH BRITAIN

It wasn't just the problems at sea that kept Madison up at night. As the new nation continued to push west, frontiersmen settled onto land that belonged to Native American tribes. Trouble was brewing between the new settlers and the native people. Britain took advantage of the tension by arming the Indian nations and advising them to fight for their land. While it seemed on the surface that the British were intervening in the best interest of the native tribes, they were using it as a front to keep U.S. expansion at bay.

Many U.S. "war hawks," or people in favor of going to war, also had their eye on Canadian territory, which belonged to Britain. Madison gave in and asked Congress for a declaration of war, which it issued on June 18, 1812.

Unfortunately, due to Jefferson's downsizing, the Army was too small to be effective. Compared to Britain's 400 warships, America had six. Their generals were clueless. Their military hierarchy was disorganized and things got ugly, fast.

FLAMBÉED

The War of 1812 started badly for the young nation. In the first month of war, American soldiers were forced to surrender Detroit (in the Michigan Territory) to a much smaller British and Native American force. And that was just the beginning.

Thomas Jefferson once said that a successful invasion of Quebec, Canada, was a "mere matter of marching." He was wrong. When the troops invaded later that year, an underprepared and poorly trained military suffered one embarrassing defeat after the next. To top it all off, the War of 1812 (which actually lasted until 1815) included the Brits setting fire to the White House. It's said they even ate Madison's still-warm dinner before torching the place.

THE WAR FOR INDEPENDENCE: PART TWO

Despite all that had gone wrong, there was one huge victory Madison could hang his hat on—the Battle of New Orleans where future president Andrew Jackson trounced the redcoats. It happened two weeks after the Treaty of Ghent was signed in December 1814, which officially ended the war, but a win was a win.

Actually, the treaty put everything back the way it was and didn't address the original problems of sailors and settlers! People took it as a victory, though, and in many people's eyes, Madison had won what some considered a second War of Independence.

ON-KEY

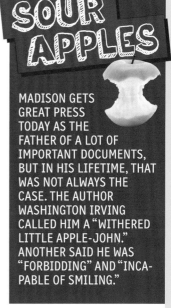

SOUR APPLES

MADISON GETS GREAT PRESS TODAY AS THE FATHER OF A LOT OF IMPORTANT DOCUMENTS, BUT IN HIS LIFETIME, THAT WAS NOT ALWAYS THE CASE. THE AUTHOR WASHINGTON IRVING CALLED HIM A "WITHERED LITTLE APPLE-JOHN." ANOTHER SAID HE WAS "FORBIDDING" AND "INCAPABLE OF SMILING."

The victory of the War of 1812 boosted American spirits and birthed the most famous song in the country—the national anthem. Francis Scott Key spent his night stuck on a British boat during a 25-hour bombardment of Fort McHenry in Baltimore, Maryland. When dawn came, he realized both he and the flag survived. Victory! To embrace the beauty, he wrote new words to an old British tune. "The Star-Spangled Banner" wasn't officially adopted as the national anthem until 1931, but everyone agreed it was catchy the minute Key wrote it.

ALL OF THE FEELINGS

With the end of the war, the future looked bright. People felt Britain had finally gotten the message to stay out of the U.S. Madison's popularity soared with the Era of Good Feelings he left behind. Everyone was feeling patriotic.

Madison left office knowing the economy was great, conflict with Britain had ended, and his hand-picked successor was taking office.

★ **TERM** 1817 to 1825
★ **PARTY** Democratic-Republican
★ **NICKNAME** The Last Cocked Hat
★ **CLAIM TO FAME** The Monroe Doctrine
★ **BORN** Westmoreland County, Virginia
★ **FIRST LADY** Elizabeth Monroe
(married 1786 to 1830)

"The American continents ..
are henceforth not to be considered
as subjects for future colonization
by any European power."

James Monroe

A CAPITAL CAPITAL Besides Washington, Monroe is the only other U.S. president with a whole country's capital named after him: Monrovia, Liberia.

James Monroe was part of the old Virginia boys' club with his pals Thomas Jefferson and James Madison. He played a pivotal part in both presidencies—helping negotiate the Louisiana Purchase for Jefferson and organizing Madison's War Department.

Monroe came into office riding the high of the Era of Good Feelings from the War of 1812. Unfortunately, those good feelings did not last.

NOBODY PANIC

It all started off well enough, but the nation's good feelings started to show signs of fizzling two years into Monroe's presidency with the Panic of 1819, which was an economic crisis where banks failed and many people could no longer afford to live in their homes. Many people were unemployed.

Monroe thought it was not his job to intervene. That's not what presidents did in the 19th century— he did not think the federal government should get involved. He figured it was just a business cycle that would eventually end. It did finally end in 1823, but the Panic hurt many Americans, and those people started to blame the banks.

UNPROMISING COMPROMISING

It wasn't just the Panic that started to weigh on the fast-growing nation. More territories wanted to be states, including Missouri and Maine, but no one could decide if the new states should allow slavery. Monroe was concerned that slavery had a bad influence on the country, even though he was a slave owner himself.

Over the next two years, he let Congress duke it out over the touchy subject of slavery. They finally settled on a compromise. Among other things, the Missouri Compromise let Missouri join as a slave state while Maine joined as a free state. But this made both sides unhappy.

MONROE ONCE DEFENDED HIMSELF WITH FIRE TONGS AFTER A DISAGREEMENT WITH HIS SECRETARY OF TREASURY!

ouch!

FREE AND SLAVE AREAS
AFTER
THE MISSOURI COMPROMISE, 1820

Greetings from FLORIDA USA

BRAVING BULLETS

AS A YOUNG COLLEGE STUDENT, MONROE LEFT SCHOOL, LOOTED THE BRITISH GOVERNOR'S PALACE FOR WEAPONS FOR THE VIRGINIA MILITIA, AND JOINED THE CONTINENTAL ARMY LED BY THE GREAT MAN HIMSELF, GEORGE WASHINGTON. AT THE BATTLE OF TRENTON DURING THE REVOLUTIONARY WAR, MONROE CHARGED INTO BRITISH CANNON FIRE AND TOOK A MUSKET BALL TO THE SHOULDER.

WATERFRONT PROPERTY

Monroe had his eye on bigger and better things for America. After all, they had (sort of) beat Britain again in the War of 1812, so why stop now? Relations with Spain had been shaky for a while, and the Spanish-owned Florida Territory looked ripe for the picking. Additionally, slave owners in the South were frustrated that their slaves were escaping to hide out in the Florida swamps, and the Native Americans were encouraging them to run away. Posses of Seminole and Creek warriors kept raiding settlements in Georgia, so Monroe sent Andrew Jackson, the hero of the War of 1812, to stop the raids.

Jackson did stop the raids, and then some. He invaded Florida, overthrew the Spanish governor, blew up a fort, and executed two British citizens he insisted were encouraging the Indians. Monroe stood behind his general, and Spain got the hint: The United States wanted Florida. Spain signed a treaty selling Florida to the U.S. for five million dollars in exchange for the U.S.'s promise to leave Texas alone.

TALK THE TALK

Now that they had successfully gone up against Spain, Americans decided they didn't want Europe sniffing around anymore. To keep Florida safe, Monroe and his secretary of state, John Quincy

Adams, came up with a bold strategy. While giving an address to Congress, Monroe said Europe was not welcome in the Western Hemisphere anymore: America would handle this side of the globe. In other words: Stay out!

The rest of the world thought it was just tough talk since America was still a pipsqueak on the power scale, but it sounded impressive. Monroe set the precedent for how the U.S. would deal with its neighbors in North and South America. Twenty years later, the policy was named the Monroe Doctrine.

PARTY TIME

At the start of Monroe's second term, he made the wise decision to fill his Cabinet with the best and brightest people. The problem came later when they all decided they wanted to be the next head honcho. Under Monroe's watch, the Federalist Party died. Eventually, two new parties were formed: the Democrats and the Whigs. Democrats like Andrew Jackson believed that the states should have more control than the federal government, and the Whigs believed in more power for the federal government.

all aboard!

PRESIDENTIAL PRECEDENTS

MONROE WAS THE FIRST PRESIDENT TO:
★ HAVE AN OUTDOOR INAUGURATION
★ LISTEN TO THE U.S. MARINE BAND PLAY AT HIS INAUGURATION
★ SAIL ON A STEAMBOAT
★ HAVE A KID GET MARRIED AT THE WHITE HOUSE

QUESTIONABLE TABLE MANNERS

DURING A FORMAL STATE DINNER, MONROE INVITED DIPLOMATS FROM FRANCE AND BRITAIN (ENEMY COUNTRIES) TO THE WHITE HOUSE. THINGS GOT A LITTLE WILD. THE BRITISH DIPLOMAT ACCUSED THE FRENCH DIPLOMAT OF BITING HIS THUMB, WHICH IS A BIG BRITISH INSULT. ONE THING LED TO ANOTHER, INSULTS FLEW, AND SWORDS WERE DRAWN. MONROE SUPPOSEDLY HAD TO BRANDISH HIS OWN SWORD AND STEP BETWEEN THEM TO STOP THE FIGHT!

6TH PRESIDENT

John Quincy Adams

OF THE U.S.A.

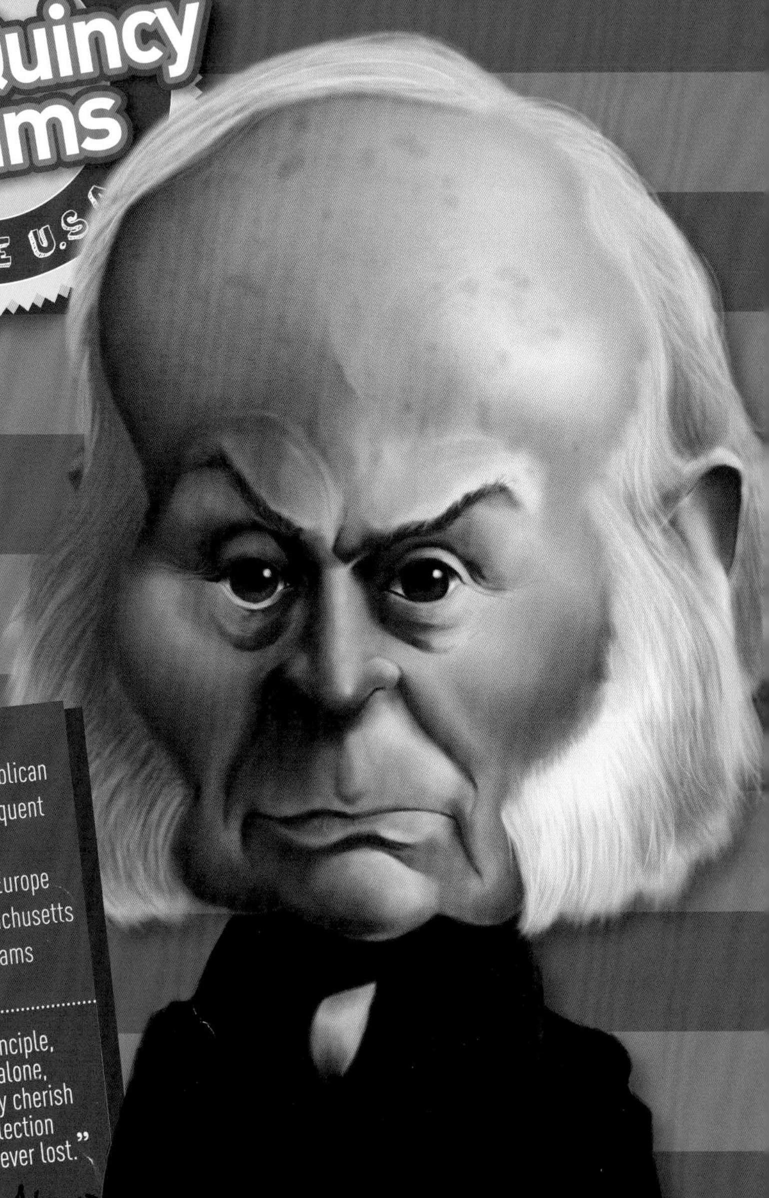

★ **TERM** 1825 to 1829

★ **PARTY** Democratic-Republican

★ **NICKNAME** Old Man Eloquent

★ **CLAIM TO FAME** Keeping the peace with Europe

★ **BORN** Braintree, Massachusetts

★ **FIRST LADY** Louisa Adams (married 1797 to 1848)

"Always vote for principle, though you may vote alone, and you may cherish the sweetest reflection that your vote is never lost."

John Quincy Adams

CHIPPED OFF Besides his name, John Quincy Adams had so much in common with his father, John Adams, that one historian called him a "chip off the old family glacier."

JOHN QUINCY ADAMS KEPT HIS PET ALLIGATOR IN THE EAST ROOM OF THE WHITE HOUSE.

chomp

Adams was a very successful politician, and an outstanding secretary of state, but his years in the White House were filled with conflict, and historians have not rated his presidency as a great success.

THE ADAMS FAMILY

John Quincy Adams was the first son of a president to become president, and the apple did not fall far from the tree. Like his father, he was known for being exceptionally smart, but uncompromising and not always popular with his peers. Historians believe it was this rigidness that sealed the deal for both father and son only serving one term in office.

ELECTION REJECTION

Adams's presidency was fraught with problems from the start. He's the only president who lost both the popular and electoral vote during the election! None of the four candidates had enough to win out-right, so the House of Representatives picked the winner, which was Adams, even though Andrew Jackson had won more votes!

The losers claimed Adams made a backroom deal with Henry Clay, promising Clay the position of secretary of state if the influential Clay was able to swing the House of Representatives to vote for him. Many called it a corrupt bargain. While these claims were never proven, it is certain that the accusations haunted Adams. They even resulted in a duel between Adams's secretary of state and a senator!

SECRET OFFICE

John Quincy Adams installed the first pool table so he could rack up billiards balls whenever he wanted.

ADAMS WAS A FIRM BELIEVER IN THE EARLY BIRD GETTING THE WORM. IN THE SUMMER, HE WAS UP BY 4:15 A.M. FOR HIS DAILY SWIM—WHICH HE LIKED TO DO NAKED. YES, ADAMS SKINNY-DIPPED IN THE POTOMAC RIVER. HE WAS ALSO THE FIRST PRES-IDENT TO HAVE HIS PIC-TURE TAKEN. BUT DON'T WORRY, HE WORE CLOTHES FOR THAT.

HOW NOT TO MAKE FRIENDS

Everyone knew Adams was smart. He was so smart that he knew it was better for the country to give government jobs to people who deserved them—not just because they were friends. That kind of thing didn't help keep friends very long in politics.

SKY-HIGH DREAMS

In his first annual address to Congress, Adams pro-posed a canal system, roads that weren't wagon-wheel ruts, a national university, and observatories to study the stars.

He called his observatories his "lighthouses of the sky." To his opponents, it seemed more like pie in the sky. To them, he was acting beyond the scope of his power—especially when he planned to finance it all with a high federal tariff.

THE ORIGINAL CINCINNATI OBSERVATORY, THE FIRST PUBLIC OBSERVATORY IN THE U.S., WAS LOCATED ON MT. ADAMS.

THE ABOMINABLE TARIFF-MAN

Tariffs are taxes on imported and exported goods. High tariffs are supposed to protect American-made products by raising the prices on foreign trade, but they didn't impact states equally. Parts of the industrial North loved the idea because it would raise the price of British goods, making people more likely to buy products made in their own factories instead. But the more agricultural South didn't like it because it would raise the prices of goods they didn't manufacture. It would also make other countries like Great Britain not want to buy as much of their cotton, hurting their exports.

Congress made Adams choose between a really strict tariff or no tariff at all. Adams chose the tariff. The South called the bill the Tariff of Abominations. The divide deepened between the North and the South—already at odds over slavery—and Adams's enemies blamed him for the whole mess.

CAN'T WIN

Adams's enemies made his life miserable. Historians call them anti-intellectuals, and they did everything they could to make Adams's job harder, including taking issue with every move he made. They magnified his blunders and mocked his intelligence. In the end, they won by keeping Adams from accomplishing anything and shooing him out of office after only four years.

Adams's presidency was bookended by another low-blow, dirty election. Just like dad in 1801, John Quincy Adams boycotted the winner's inauguration and refused to attend.

CHAMPION OF THE LITTLE GUY

After his presidency, John Quincy Adams represented Massachusetts in the House of Representatives. The next 17 years made him a legend in Congress. He continued to vote for what he believed was best for the nation. His conscience made him stand up to slavery, stick by his desire for advancements in science, and defend Africans who'd mutinied at sea and killed the white sailors taking them to slavery.

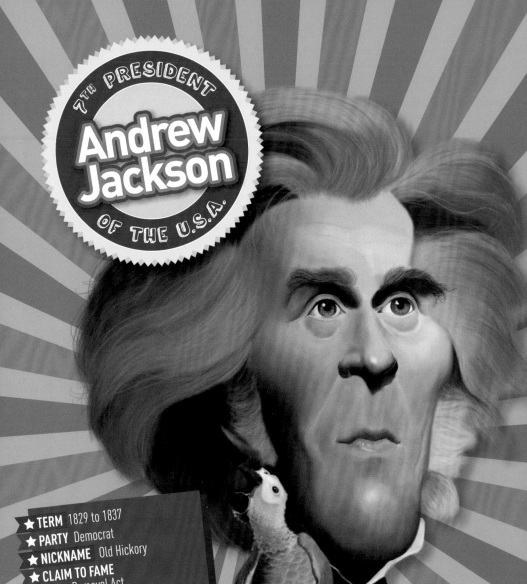

7TH PRESIDENT
Andrew Jackson
OF THE U.S.A.

★ **TERM** 1829 to 1837
★ **PARTY** Democrat
★ **NICKNAME** Old Hickory
★ **CLAIM TO FAME**
  Indian Removal Act
★ **BORN** Waxhaw area, along the
  North Carolina–South Carolina border
★ **SPOUSE** Rachel Jackson
  (married 1794 to 1828)

"The bank, Mr. Van Buren, is trying
to kill me but I will kill it."

Andrew Jackson

PARTY LIKE A PRESIDENT There's no party like a Jackson party! At one,
his friends devoured a 1,400-pound (635-kg) cheese wheel in two hours flat. The devastation left ▶▶▶

Andrew Jackson was super patriotic. It all started when a British officer ordered a teenage Jackson to clean the soldier's boots during the Revolutionary War. Even in his youth, Jackson was not the sort to take that kneeling down with a dirty rag. He refused, and the officer drew a sword and slashed Jackson on both his hand and his head, leaving behind permanent scars.

FIGHTING WORDS

Jackson always felt he was on the right side of justice, and never backed down from confrontation. He became a legend during the War of 1812 when he crushed the British at the Battle of New Orleans. (Of course, the battle happened two weeks after the peace treaty was signed, but it was still a moral victory.) People felt he'd brought honor to the young country.

President Monroe might have gotten more than he bargained for when he sent Jackson to invade Spanish-held Florida in 1818 to stamp out uprisings that plagued the region. Jackson claimed it was necessary to take control of the area to protect white settlers from attacks by Native Americans, but he killed two British subjects and many Native Americans in the process.

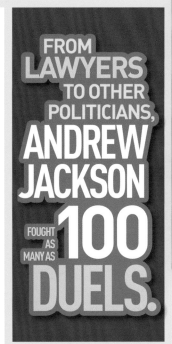

FROM **LAWYERS** TO OTHER POLITICIANS, **ANDREW JACKSON** FOUGHT AS MANY AS **100 DUELS.**

CLEANING THE CABINETS

As president, Jackson wasn't about to sit around letting things stay the same. He'd accused John Quincy Adams of corruption; now he intended to make things right. Jackson hadn't pitched himself as a man of the people for nothing!

He dismissed all of the men in Cabinet positions that had been appointed by Adams, and hired his friends instead.

1,400 pounds
(635 kg)

greasy stains on the carpet for years.

&@#%

WHY HE'S WEIRD

Andrew Jackson had a temper, and his pet bird apparently picked up on his habits. At the president's funeral, his parrot, Poll, started cursing so loudly that the bird had to be escorted away from the ceremony.

SPOILED SYSTEM

As for the rest of the government jobs, Jackson wanted to make things fairer by rotating people, but he usually gave those jobs to friends, too. When he gave jobs to unqualified friends it created a whole new beast: the spoils system. This is where the winners in politics give their supporters government jobs as a thank-you. One "friend" even made off with more than a million dollars in government money!

TAXING TAXES

Meanwhile, John Quincy Adams's Tariff of Abominations was still causing problems between the states. Representatives in South Carolina weren't joking when they declared it unconstitutional. They said they wouldn't collect tariff monies and threatened to leave the Union over it, and even raised an army to defend themselves!

Not on Jackson's watch! He loved America too much to see it split up, so he threatened South Carolina with the U.S. Army. They finally settled on a compromise. Over the next nine years, the tariff would be lowered. Everyone backed off the tax trigger.

A TERRIBLE TRAIL

Jackson's next goal was to pass a controversial bill that left a big scar on the history of the country. Relations with the Native Americans were as rocky as ever, and in Jackson's mind, the only way to keep white settlers safe was to move Native Americans west of the Mississippi River. He introduced and implemented the Indian Removal Act of 1830, which was passed by Congress. This act forced the relocation of tribes out of the southeastern states. A few tribes went peacefully, but most did not.

Jackson claimed it was for the Native Americans' own protection and the preservation of their culture, but eventually removal agents used chains, guns, and fear to force the tribes west to land that would be theirs "forever," Oklahoma. An estimated 4,000 Cherokees died on the forced, grueling march that earned the name the Trail of Tears.

CLOSE CALL

Andrew Jackson was the target of the first ever attempted presidential assassination. While the president was leaving a funeral, a housepainter claiming to be the king of England walked up to Jackson and fired point blank—except the gun wouldn't shoot. The painter threw that away and pulled out a second pistol. It also seized up.

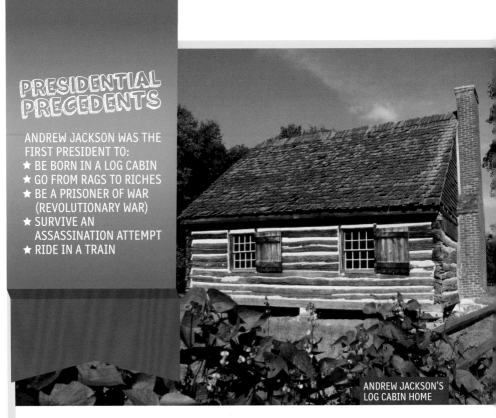

PRESIDENTIAL PRECEDENTS

ANDREW JACKSON WAS THE FIRST PRESIDENT TO:
* ★ BE BORN IN A LOG CABIN
* ★ GO FROM RAGS TO RICHES
* ★ BE A PRISONER OF WAR (REVOLUTIONARY WAR)
* ★ SURVIVE AN ASSASSINATION ATTEMPT
* ★ RIDE IN A TRAIN

ANDREW JACKSON'S LOG CABIN HOME

Jackson, then 67 years old, defended himself by beating the would-be assassin with his cane until the man was wrestled away. When someone tried the two pistols later, both fired fine.

MONEY MISTAKES

Jackson used his Cabinet to rally support for things he wanted done and things he wanted undone. One thing he wanted removed was the Bank of the United States. He hated the bank, and especially debt. He is actually the only president to ever pay off the national debt, which he did by vetoing spending bills and selling off government-owned land out West.

Jackson believed that the Bank of the U.S. had too much power, and favored the wealthy elite over the common people. To achieve his goals, Jackson went on the attack and vetoed the bank's re-charter bill. While he was right that the bank did tend to favor the rich, he failed to realize that it also stabilized the economy. The eventual depression wouldn't be his problem, but it would be partly his fault.

NOT GIVING A FIG FOR WHIGS

It didn't take long for Jackson's enemies to band together. They called him "King Andrew" and referred to themselves as Whigs, after the British political party that hated kingly tyranny.

PARTY POOPER

JACKSON CONSIDERED HIM-SELF A PRESIDENT FOR THE PEOPLE—BECAUSE HE WAS THE PEOPLE. HE WAS BORN INTO POVERTY AND WORKED HIS WAY INTO HIGH SOCIETY. SOME THOUGHT HE BROUGHT "LOW" SOCIETY STANDARDS WITH HIM TO THE WHITE HOUSE. JACKSON'S INAUGURATION PARTY WAS AN OPEN HOUSE KIND OF AFFAIR. ACCORDING TO A SENATOR, IT WAS A "STREAM OF MUD AND FILTH," AND HIS WELL-WISHERS WERE NOT EXACTLY THE TYPE OF CROWD USED TO BEING ENTERTAINED IN THE WHITE HOUSE. THEY BROKE, SLASHED, AND DEVOURED THEIR WAY THROUGH FOOD AND FURNI-TURE UNTIL THEY WERE EVENTUALLY LURED ONTO THE LAWN. JACKSON HIM-SELF ESCAPED THROUGH THE BACK DOOR!

NEAT-O VETO

Vetoes used to be for things the president found unconstitutional. Jackson thought that was silly. All that power with a simple "no" was right at his feather-tipped pen! Jackson vetoed 12 bills, which doesn't sound like a lot to us, but previous presidents had vetoed only nine bills—in total.

IMPORTATION NATION

Jackson was not afraid to stand up to anyone, even powerful countries. This included the French when he demanded they make overdue payments on a ship they damaged. He also expanded American commerce by signing treaties with Britain, and Siam (now Thailand)—the first with an Asian nation—which increased exports and imports.

LIKE JEFFERSON, LIKE JACKSON

Even though Jackson wanted less government, he also ended up expanding the powers of the presidency. He even expanded democracy for some while destroying it for others.

Despite his temper, Jackson was smart and an optimist. He believed people would ultimately do the right thing, so he encour-aged them to vote and be a part of democ-racy. While many of his actions as president are controversial, he was pivotal in shaping the young nation.

8TH PRESIDENT
Martin Van Buren
OF THE U.S.A.

- ★ **TERM** 1837 to 1841
- ★ **PARTY** Democrat
- ★ **NICKNAME** Little Magician
- ★ **CLAIM TO FAME** Bringing the term "OK" into popularity
- ★ **BORN** Kinderhook, New York
- ★ **SPOUSE** Hannah Van Buren (married 1807 to 1819)

"It's easier to do a job right than to explain why you didn't."

M Van Buren

MADE IN AMERICA
Because he was born after the Revolution, Van Buren was the first president not born a British citizen.

V an Buren sweated his way up the political ladder and got his taste for politics early in life. Some say the mingling with different sorts of people is where Van Buren picked up his diplomatic skills and shrewdness in negotiating. His father owned a tavern, which was frequented by the likes of Alexander Hamilton, a Founding Father, and Aaron Burr, the third vice president.

Despite his humble beginnings and the fact that Van Buren was Andrew Jackson's handpicked successor, the opposing party of the time, the Whigs, painted polite Van Buren as too fancy for the people. Eventually he lost reelection to William Henry Harrison, who, ironically, actually was from a wealthy Virginia family.

TIGER TROUBLE The Sultan of Oman once gave Van Buren two tiger cubs. He kept them in the White House for a while, much to Congress's ▶▶▶

TANKING BANKS

Van Buren had an uphill battle from day one. Jackson's financial policies helped cause the worst economic depression to date only a few weeks after Van Buren's inauguration. Instead of blaming Jackson's policies, Van Buren pointed the finger at greedy rich men and said that the government should store its money in an independent treasury. Unfortunately for Van Buren, many people pointed their fingers at *him* for the economic downturn. Eventually Congress approved his idea for an independent treasury in 1840.

OKEY-DOKEY!

DID YOU KNOW THAT YOU HAVE VAN BUREN TO THANK FOR POPULARIZING THE TERM "OK"? WELL, AT LEAST PARTIALLY. DURING HIS PRESIDENCY, VAN BUREN'S SUPPORTERS RALLIED CROWDS WITH ROUSING CHORUSES OF "O.K." THE LETTERS STOOD FOR VAN BUREN'S NICKNAME, OLD KINDERHOOK, BUT THEY ALSO REFERRED TO THE EXPRESSION "ALL CORRECT." THE TERM "OK" TOOK OFF— AND STUCK.

MARTIN VAN BUREN IS THE **ONLY** PRESIDENT TO HAVE **ENGLISH AS HIS SECOND LANGUAGE.** LITTLE MAARTEN GREW UP **SPEAKING DUTCH.**

"MARTIN VAN RUIN"

Besides some people blaming him for the Panic of 1837, shortly after which he got the nickname "Martin Van Ruin," Van Buren was grappling with foreign affairs issues. Maine and British Canada were squabbling over borders. Instead of sending in troops, Van Buren sent in diplomats. The good news was that the diplomats were successful and a treaty was negotiated. The bad news was that many people felt he should have gone to war instead. Some people started to think he was too soft.

Since he wasn't war-hungry enough and couldn't fix the economy, the Democrats and even Jackson himself left Van Buren behind.

WHY HE'S WEIRD!

VAN BUREN WAS ALSO NICKNAMED THE "SLY FOX" AND "LITTLE MAGICIAN" BECAUSE HE WAS KNOWN FOR DOING FAVORS FOR PEOPLE IN RETURN FOR GETTING WHAT HE WANTED. TODAY, THIS BEHAVIOR IS OFTEN THOUGHT OF AS COMMONPLACE FOR POLITICIANS.

displeasure. Eventually, at the urging of Congress, he took them to a zoo.

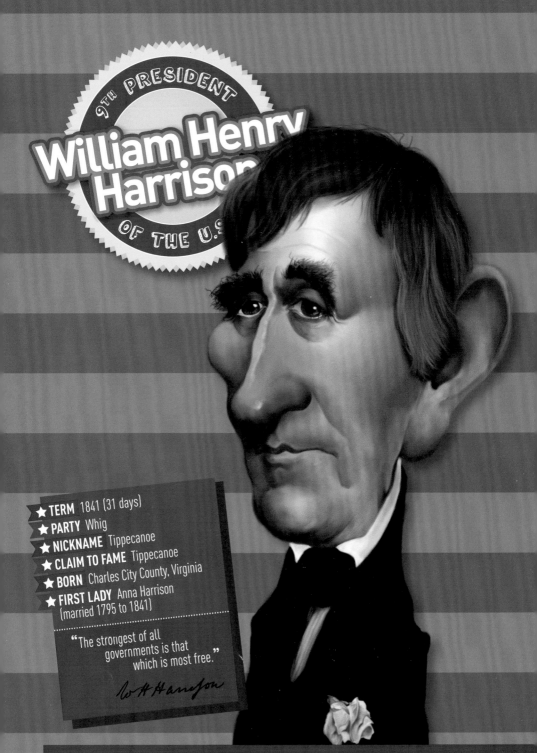

William Henry Harrison

★ **TERM** 1841 (31 days)
★ **PARTY** Whig
★ **NICKNAME** Tippecanoe
★ **CLAIM TO FAME** Tippecanoe
★ **BORN** Charles City County, Virginia
★ **FIRST LADY** Anna Harrison (married 1795 to 1841)

"The strongest of all governments is that which is most free."

W H Harrison

SERIOUS SWAG Today, candidates provide buttons and bumper stickers to campaign. In 1840, Harrison handed out ceramic pitchers with his face on them! He wanted to appear ▶▶▶

Before he was president, Harrison was governor of the Indiana Territory and told to get land for the U.S. The tricks and tactics he used were not nice. (Sometimes he only offered a penny for 200 acres [18 ha] of land!)

When the brilliant Chief Tecumseh united the Native American tribes in resistance, it led to a showdown at Tippecanoe in 1811. It was Harrison versus the Prophet (Tecumseh's brother), and Harrison won. Still, it took Harrison two more years to defeat the chief, but he instantly got Tippecanoe as a nickname—and as marketing material.

VOTE FOR TIPPECANOE!

Harrison snowballed his military might into a run for the White House. His run for office epitomized a modern campaign, complete with advertising, slogans, and free stuff.

And when Van Buren supporters accused Harrison of being a simpleton with a taste for hard cider, instead of getting defensive, Harrison used that to his advantage. Harrison remade his image, and that of his running mate, John Tyler, as down-to-earth men of the people.

THE HERO OF TIPPECANOE

CATCHING COLD

Harrison probably didn't listen to his mother. He went to his rain-drenched inauguration without a coat or hat. Instead of making it snappy, he spoke for almost two hours. The highlights of the speech boiled down to his promising to do the opposite of Andrew Jackson and to never run for president again.

It was one promise he kept. He caught a cold and died a month later.

HARRISON WAITED UNTIL HIS **GIRLFRIEND'S DAD** WAS OUT OF TOWN BEFORE **SECRETLY MARRYING HER.**

WHY HE'S WEIRD!

IT TOOK A HUNDRED YEARS, BUT PEOPLE STARTED TO NOTICE PRESIDENTS ELECTED IN 20-YEAR INTERVALS SEEMED TO DIE IN OFFICE. THEY CALLED IT THE "CURSE OF TECUMSEH" AFTER THE NATIVE AMERICAN CHIEF. APPARENTLY, LEGEND HAS IT THAT TECUMSEH'S BROTHER PUT A CURSE ON ONE PRESIDENT EVERY GENERATION.

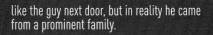

like the guy next door, but in reality he came from a prominent family.

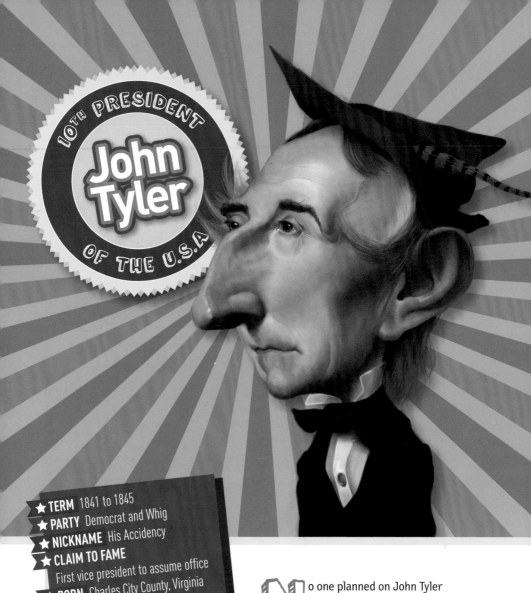

10TH PRESIDENT John Tyler OF THE U.S.A.

★ **TERM** 1841 to 1845
★ **PARTY** Democrat and Whig
★ **NICKNAME** His Accidency
★ **CLAIM TO FAME**
First vice president to assume office
★ **BORN** Charles City County, Virginia
★ **FIRST LADIES** Letitia Christian Tyler
(married 1813 to 1842), Julia Gardiner
Tyler (married 1844 to 1862)

" I, as president, shall be
responsible for my administration. "

John Tyler

No one planned on John Tyler becoming president, and once he was there, many felt he didn't deserve the office. After just one month in office, President William Henry Harrison died—the first president to die in office. Then the public was full of questions. Was Tyler actually president now or was he just a decoration? Congress turned to the Constitution for answers, but came up empty-handed.

RETURN TO SENDER During his term, Tyler received death threats and hate mail addressed to "Acting President Tyler." He returned them unopened.

Tyler had 15 kids— the most of any president!

LARGELY IN CHARGE

Tyler decided to silence all this "accidental president" talk by being formally inaugurated as president the day after President Harrison died. He initially kept Harrison's entire Cabinet, but let them know that he was the only man in charge.

POWER PLAY

Tyler's Cabinet didn't like him, and the feeling was mutual. His political party, the Whigs, wanted to bring the Bank of the U.S. back, but Tyler, a man in favor of states' rights, thought the bank would be too power-ful and was unconstitutional, so he vetoed it. The Cabinet resigned in protest, except for the secretary of state, Daniel Webster. (Webster wanted to, but he was in the middle of border negotiations between Maine and British Canada.)

WHIGGING OUT

By the end of his term, the Whigs had ousted Tyler from their party and even tried to impeach him. (The impeachment didn't pass.) His last day in office was busy. He gave Florida statehood days after he engineered the annex-ation of Texas. As a thanks, Congress overrode his veto on military spending—Congress's first override of a president's veto.

WHY HE'S WEIRD!

JOHN TYLER HAD A SOFT SPOT FOR REBELS. HE EVEN NAMED HIS PLANTATION SHERWOOD FOREST AFTER ROBIN HOOD. SO IT'S NOT THAT SURPRISING HE'S THE ONLY FORMER PRESIDENT TO JOIN THE CONFEDERACY. HE WAS A VIRGINIAN AND STAYED LOYAL TO HIS STATE. HE CONSIDERED HIMSELF A POLITICAL OUTLAW, JUST LIKE ROBIN HOOD.

DANCE PARTNERS

At least one thing was going right: Webster's border negotiation. The Webster-Ashburton Treaty of 1842 finally drew the line between Maine and British Canada.

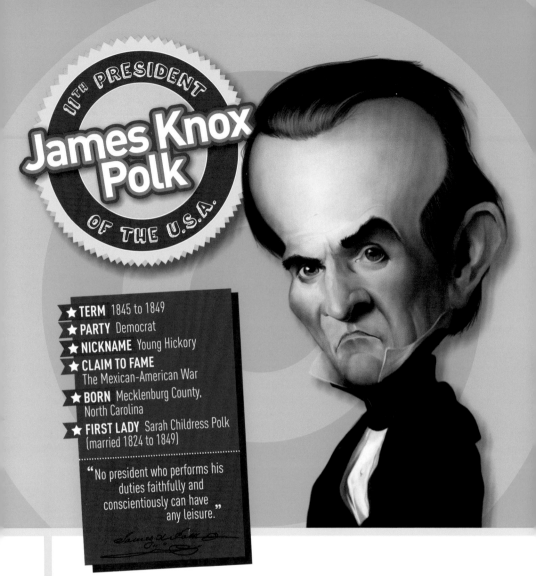

11TH PRESIDENT

James Knox Polk

OF THE U.S.A.

★ **TERM** 1845 to 1849
★ **PARTY** Democrat
★ **NICKNAME** Young Hickory
★ **CLAIM TO FAME**
  The Mexican-American War
★ **BORN** Mecklenburg County,
  North Carolina
★ **FIRST LADY** Sarah Childress Polk
  (married 1824 to 1849)

"No president who performs his
duties faithfully and
conscientiously can have
any leisure."

During his day, Polk's opponents campaigned with the slogan, "Who is James K. Polk?" These days, historians say he's an important link between Jackson and Lincoln's presidencies. He was given the nickname Young Hickory because he hero-worshipped Andrew Jackson and largely agreed with him on policy. When Polk took office, he had four objectives: lower tariffs, fix the banks, expand territory, and address slavery.

TANGO-ING TARIFFS

Polk worked hard to reduce tariffs, or taxes on imported or exported goods. Like many other wealthy Southern planters, he thought high tariffs favored Northern industry. His tariff plan passed Congress. Next, Polk tackled the banking system.

TOUGH GUY Polk underwent serious surgery when he was 17—while he was awake and without any germ-killing antiseptic!

BANK BREAK-DANCE

Even though he idolized Jackson, Polk learned a lesson from the economic depression that resulted in part from Jackson's bank policies. Only a year after adopting Van Buren's independent treasury, which kept the federal government's funds separate and safe from the states, Congress killed it again. Polk wanted it back to avoid another depression. The treasury easily passed and survived until 1921.

WALTZING WEST

Even in his inaugural address, Polk made it clear that he planned to expand U.S. territory. And he did. During his presidency, over a million square miles (2.6 million sq km) were added to the U.S. Folks called it Manifest Destiny—the belief that Americans were destined to spread out and settle across North America.

WHY HE'S WEIRD!

ONCE, POLK'S WIFE AGREED TO A WHITE HOUSE PERFORMANCE BY A JUGGLER, AND CONVINCED HER HUSBAND TO ATTEND. APPARENTLY POLK WASN'T IMPRESSED AND SAID HE'D RATHER BE WORKING!

SUPPOSEDLY, POLK LEARNED TO RIDE A HORSE BEFORE HE LEARNED TO WALK!

TO MEXICO!

President Tyler had annexed Texas, which means he formally took control of new territory (that Mexico still believed it owned). Polk was on board with that, but Mexico wasn't. Polk sent in troops to the disputed territory, bloodshed eventually occurred, and Congress declared war. After two years, U.S. forces captured Mexico City. Eventually Mexico agreed to sell the land from California to the Rio Grande (what is today Arizona, Nevada,

Utah, California, and most of New Mexico) for
$15 million.

TODAY, POLK IS CONSIDERED ONE OF THE HARDEST-WORKING PRESIDENTS OF ALL TIME. HE WORKED ABOUT 12 HOURS A DAY! AT AGE 49, HE WAS THE YOUNGEST PRESIDENT YET, BUT DON'T LET THAT FOOL YOU—HISTORIANS SAY THAT, CONTRARY TO HIS AGE, POLK HAD A SOMBER, SERIOUS DISPOSITION. HE AND HIS WIFE WERE VERY RELIGIOUS AND EVEN BANNED DANCING FROM WHITE HOUSE RECEPTIONS. SUPPOSEDLY, AT HIS INAUGURATION, ALL MUSIC AND DANCING STOPPED WHILE THEY WERE THERE AND STARTED UP AGAIN AFTER THEY LEFT!

SLAVE STATES VERSUS FREE STATES

Acquiring all that new territory presented Polk with some serious problems. People were hotly debating which states should become free states (where slavery was illegal) and which should become slave states (where slavery was legal). If there were more slave states, the fear was that the pro-slavery South would control Congress. If there were more free states, the antislavery North would control Congress. The combined issues of slavery and western expansion made it clear that big, ugly cracks were continuing to spread, splitting across America.

STATE OF CONTAGION

Polk is known for keeping all of his campaign promises. His last promise was not to run for a second term. He kept it, too, even though many historians say he was so popular he could have won again. Just months into retirement, he took a tour of the Southern states and contracted cholera, a deadly bacterial infection. He had requested before his death that the family's slaves be freed upon his wife's death.

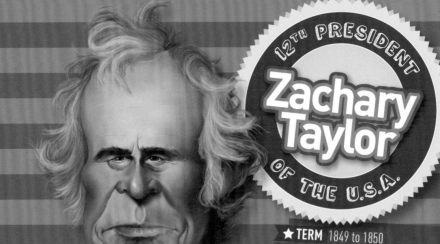

12TH PRESIDENT
Zachary Taylor
OF THE U.S.A.

★ **TERM** 1849 to 1850
★ **PARTY** Whig
★ **NICKNAME** Old Rough-and-Ready
★ **CLAIM TO FAME** Mexican War hero
★ **BORN** Barboursville, Virginia
★ **FIRST LADY** Margaret Taylor (married 1810 to 1850)

" I am not a party candidate and if elected, can not be president of a party but the president of the whole people. "

Zachary Taylor

TAYLOR WAS A CHAMPION SPITTER WHO COULD HIT A MARK SIX (1.8 m) **FEET AWAY.**

Zachary Taylor was no politician. He had never even voted! The Army general spent the last 40 years on the business end of a bayonet, fighting in every conflict from the War of 1812 to the Mexican-American War. At the time, he was hailed as a hero of the Mexican-American War

PRESIDENTIAL PIZZAZZ During campaigns, Taylor would wear a laid-back assortment of mismatched clothing. And that didn't stop after he became president!

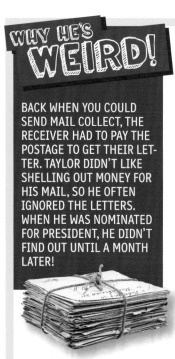

and hugely popular with the public. People thought if he ran for president he had a great chance of winning. But there was one problem: No one knew what his politics were. He was really an independent, but he aligned with some basic Whig principles, like having a strong and stable bank system and believing that the president should be more hands-off with Congress. The Whigs knew a winner when they saw one. They adopted him and let him run with no platform—a decision that some historians say backfired.

ROUGH AND READY TO GO

The big issue of the day was slavery. Should all that new land acquired under Polk become slave states or free? Taylor thought each new state had the right to choose. This angered Southerners and Northerners alike. Compromise was getting nowhere, and the South started talking about secession: leaving the U.S.

DEATH BY ... CHERRIES?

Taylor was a firm unionist—he believed all the states needed to stick together. He promised to personally lead the Army if the South tried leaving. He never got the chance because he died 16 months into his term.

It was the Fourth of July in D.C. After festivities under the blazing sun, Taylor kicked back with some cherries and a pitcher of milk. Hours later, cramps seized his stomach. Five days later, he was dead. To this day, historians and conspiracy theorists alike speculate on what caused the sudden death of the president. But in 1991, after running some tests, doctors are pretty sure it wasn't poison.

I'M ROUGH AND READY!

13TH PRESIDENT Millard Fillmore OF THE U.S.A.

* ★ **TERM** 1850 to 1853
* ★ **PARTY** Whig
* ★ **NICKNAME** The Accidental President
* ★ **CLAIM TO FAME** Compromising
* ★ **BORN** Summerhill, New York
* ★ **FIRST LADY** Abigail Fillmore (married 1826 to 1853)

"(A)n honorable defeat is better than a dishonorable victory."

M. Fillmore

Fillmore was born into extreme poverty. His parents couldn't afford to take care of him, so they sent him off to an apprenticeship with a clothmaker. Historians say the experience was terrible and just short of slavery. During this period, Fillmore stole books so he could teach himself to read. Even years after his presidency, Fillmore didn't embellish himself. He turned down an honorary degree from Oxford saying he didn't deserve it!

By the end of his term, Fillmore wasn't well liked.

FILLMORE ONCE PERSONALLY HELPED PUT OUT A FIRE AT THE LIBRARY OF CONGRESS!

OPEN (TRADE) DOORS
Fillmore sent the first naval expedition to Japan to forcibly open up trade relations. Before that, Japan had been closed to foreigners for three centuries!

The map shows:
WASH. TER. 1853 OPENED TO SLAVERY BY DRED SCOTT DECISION 1857

OREGON TER. 1848

CALIFORNIA ADMITTED FREE 1850

NEBRASKA TERRITORY OPENED TO SLAVERY 1854 BY KANSAS NEBRASKA BILL 1854

MINNESOTA TER.

1849 SLAVERY

UTAH TERRITORY OPENED TO SLAVERY 1850 BY COMPROMISE OF 1850

KANSAS TER. 1854

NEW MEXICO TERRITORY 1850-53

UNORGANIZED

FREE STATES

SLAVE STATES

MEXICO

30°

SLAVE AND FREE TERRITORY 1854

He had signed unpopular laws and his political party was falling apart.

A BAD COMPROMISE

Historians note Fillmore's big problem—he was a people pleaser, and that led to a lot of compromises. That sounds like a good thing, but it wasn't when the nation needed someone to lead them away from crisis. While Fillmore didn't approve of slavery himself, he thought abolishing it would lead to war. So he signed a law called the Compromise of 1850.

In that law, California became a free state and the slave trade (but not slavery) was outlawed in Washington, D.C., in exchange for the Fugitive Slave Act. Among other things, the act required every citizen to help return runaway slaves, including those in free states. Many people in free states refused, and the tensions continued to simmer.

THE PARTY'S OVER

MILLARD FILLMORE, AMERICAN CANDIDATE FOR PRESIDENT OF THE UNITED STATES.

Eventually Fillmore's political party couldn't agree on issues and it broke apart. Even though the Whigs were finished with him, Fillmore wasn't ready to be done with politics. In 1856, he accepted the nomination of the American Party, also known as the Know-Nothings, an anti-immigrant political party that had cropped up during Polk's term. They were primarily against the waves of Irish immigrants coming to America during and after the Irish potato famine. As their presidential candidate, Fillmore won exactly one state, Maryland, though he won nearly 22 percent of the popular vote.

He may be forgotten and ignored by history books, but his character was unimpeachable. He never smoked, drank, or had a scandal, and he only gambled once. There is literally no gossip for this guy!

14TH PRESIDENT
Franklin Pierce
OF THE U.S.A

★ **TERM** 1853 to 1857
★ **PARTY** Democrat
★ **NICKNAME** Handsome Frank
★ **CLAIM TO FAME** Kansas-Nebraska Act
★ **BORN** Hillsborough, New Hampshire
★ **FIRST LADY** Jane Pierce (married 1834 to 1863)

"The storm of frenzy and faction must inevitably dash itself in vain against the unshaken rock of the Constitution."

Franklin Pierce

PIERCE HAD A REPUTATION FOR BEING A HUGE GOSSIP!

Pierce was a compromise candidate. He'd gotten the nomination because he was a Northerner who supported states' rights and the right of white Southerners to own slaves. All he wanted was peace and prosperity. But his presidency started off with tragedy. Two months before he was supposed to start his new job as president, his train derailed and killed his only son. Pierce came into office heartbroken. Meanwhile, tensions were growing between the North and South and his problems with railroads weren't over yet.

TROUBLE IN KANSAS

With all that new land recently acquired, some politicians wanted a railroad to connect it all. Pierce's Northern allies in Congress wanted the railroad to run through the North and not pass through any slave states. They pressed Pierce to sign the Kansas-Nebraska Act. The act established Kansas and Nebraska as

POCKET-SIZE PRESENTS Pierce was gifted two "teacup" dogs from Japan. They were so small they could fit on a teacup saucer!

PIERCE DIDN'T KNOW MUCH ABOUT FIGHTING IN A WAR. IN HIS FIRST BATTLE OF THE MEXICAN-AMERICAN WAR, PIERCE'S HORSE STARTED BUCKING AT THE SOUND OF A CANNON, AND HE WAS THROWN INTO HIS SADDLE, CAUSING HIM TO FAINT. HE FELL OFF HIS HORSE AND INJURED HIS KNEE. THE NEXT DAY, HE WRENCHED HIS KNEE WHILE MARCHING AND FAINTED, *AGAIN*. FAINTING FRANK NEVER LIVED THAT DOWN.

official territories. More importantly, the act allowed the new territories to decide if they would allow slavery or not. Then both pro-slavery and free-soil party members (those who wanted new states to be free states) poured into Kansas, rigging elections and fighting over slavery in the new state. It was a huge disaster—and brought the nation another step closer to civil war.

ALL ABOARD

The Underground Railroad wasn't an actual train. It was a series of secret routes and safe houses leading north that people like Harriet Tubman used to help slaves escape to freedom. President Pierce condemned it and Harriet.

THE RISE OF THE REPUBLICANS

choo choo!

President Franklin Pierce didn't want to give up. He felt he could help patch things up during a second term. The Democrats said no thanks, and all the people who didn't like him or slavery started the Republican Party in 1854. Instead, the Democrats put their hope in another candidate from the North that supported slavery in the South—James Buchanan.

15TH PRESIDENT
James Buchanan
OF THE U.S.A.

★ **TERM** 1857 to 1861
★ **PARTY** Democrat
★ **NICKNAME** Old Buck
★ **CLAIM TO FAME**
The John Brown rebellion and Southern secession
★ **BORN** Cove Gap, Pennsylvania

"I am the last president of the United States!"

James Buchanan

Tensions were rising. Actual fistfights broke out in the House of Representatives, and in some states people became violent over the issue of slavery. Buchanan was supposed to bridge the divide between the North and South since he was a Northerner who liked the South and was okay with the institution of slavery. Buchanan echoed his predecessors and said states should decide for themselves.

BUCHANAN IS THE ONLY BACHELOR PRESIDENT.

PRESIDENTIAL QUIRKS Buchanan was nearsighted in one eye and farsighted in the other. This led to his habit of cocking his head to the side and closing one eye.

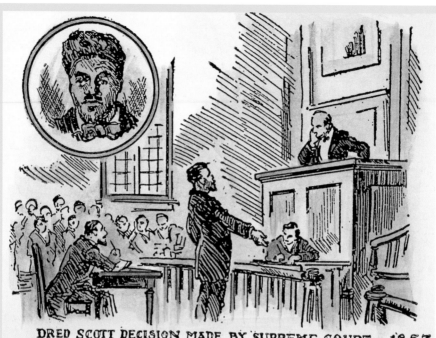

DRED SCOTT DECISION MADE BY SUPREME COURT - 1857

SUPREMELY UNFAIR

Two days after Buchanan's inauguration, the Supreme Court ruled that black people (free or slave) weren't citizens and effectively had no rights in a U.S. court of law. In what became known as the Dred Scott case, it further fueled regional tensions and continued the march to the Civil War. The court also ruled that the federal government didn't have the power to outlaw slavery in its territories. The ruling angered many Northerners.

RAIDING RADICALS

One man took matters into his own hands. John Brown was an abolitionist, which means he wanted to end slavery. Brown had previously been involved in the violence in Kansas, as he and some of his sons killed four settlers in a pro-slavery town. In 1859, he traveled to Harpers Ferry, Virginia. He wanted to take over the federal arsenal there in hopes of starting a slave uprising by distributing the weapons he captured. The plan was unsuccessful, Brown was executed, and the slave uprising didn't happen, but the incident did raise tensions even more. In many Southerners' minds, it confirmed their fears that the North really did want to invade, and it convinced Buchanan that a civil war would be the abolitionists' fault. Some historians argue that the Civil War really began with Brown. How did Buchanan respond? He repeated that the states should decide on slavery themselves.

BIG-TALKING BUCHANEERS

Buchanan vowed to serve one term and his party made him stick to his promise. But Buchanan's supporters, called Buchaneers, made things hairy at the Democratic Party's convention by disagreeing with all the nominees and delaying votes. All this infighting, among other issues, helped the still-new Republicans and their candidate—Abraham Lincoln.

LET ME OUT!

In the four months between Lincoln's election in November and his inauguration in March, seven states left the Union. To Buchanan, the secession wasn't constitutional, but forcing the states to stay in the Union wouldn't be constitutional, either. So he didn't do anything, which gave the Confederacy time to organize.

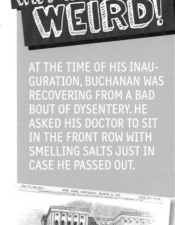

WHY HE'S WEIRD!

AT THE TIME OF HIS INAUGURATION, BUCHANAN WAS RECOVERING FROM A BAD BOUT OF DYSENTERY. HE ASKED HIS DOCTOR TO SIT IN THE FRONT ROW WITH SMELLING SALTS JUST IN CASE HE PASSED OUT.

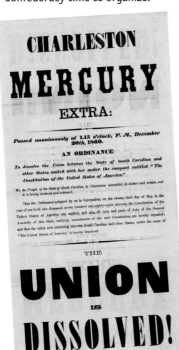

IS IT OVER YET?

Buchanan constantly hoped the Southern states would come around and realize they wanted to stay, but that would never happen with such an explosive issue.

Buchanan refused to hand over U.S. forts in the seceding states to the Confederacy.

Things were starting to take a turn for the worse, and apparently Buchanan was eager for his term to be over. According to some sources, he told Lincoln, "If you are as happy entering the White House as I am leaving it, you are a happy man indeed."

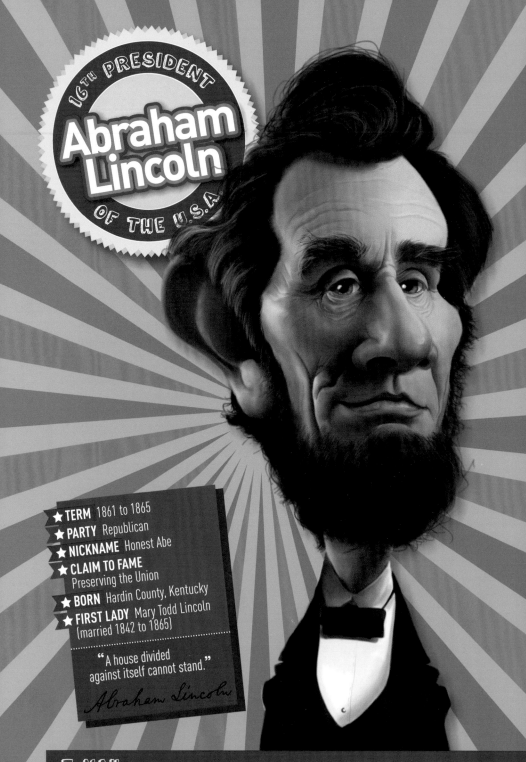

16TH PRESIDENT
Abraham Lincoln
OF THE U.S.A.

- ★ **TERM** 1861 to 1865
- ★ **PARTY** Republican
- ★ **NICKNAME** Honest Abe
- ★ **CLAIM TO FAME** Preserving the Union
- ★ **BORN** Hardin County, Kentucky
- ★ **FIRST LADY** Mary Todd Lincoln (married 1842 to 1865)

"A house divided against itself cannot stand."

Abraham Lincoln

T-MAIL Lincoln constantly needed to keep in contact with his generals, but in the days when letters were delivered by the Pony Express, communication was slow. Lincoln stuck to ▶▶▶

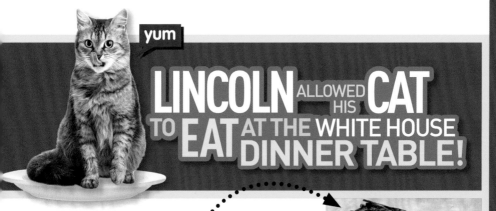

yum

LINCOLN ALLOWED HIS CAT TO EAT AT THE WHITE HOUSE DINNER TABLE!

L incoln was born in a one-room log cabin in Kentucky and had only a year of formal schooling, but that didn't stop him from educating himself. He impressed people with his intelligence and honesty throughout his life, eventually earning the nickname "Honest Abe." When he got elected, he faced the biggest crisis the young nation had ever seen. Between his election and inauguration, seven states left the Union to form the Confederate States of America, complete with their own president. To lawyer Lincoln, this was not legal. So he committed himself to bringing the country back together. The next four years were going to be one uphill battle after another.

FIRST SHOTS AT FORT SUMTER

Outgoing President Buchanan had refused to give up Fort Sumter in Charleston, South Carolina, to the Confederates. The only problem was that there were 80 soldiers trapped inside and the food was about to run out. When Lincoln took office, he needed to figure out how to get the men supplies without starting a war. He told the Confederates that he'd be sending in unarmed supply ships to feed the hungry men. On April 12, 1861, before the ships could get there, the Confederates fired on the fort. Fort Sumter surrendered to the Confederates after 33 hours of bombardment—and the Civil War officially began.

MAN OF ACTION

Lincoln moved quickly after that. Congress wasn't meeting, so he issued an executive order, which comes from the president and is as powerful as a law. He ordered the

WHY HE'S WEIRD!

ABRAHAM LINCOLN LOVED TELLING JOKES. IN FACT, WHEN EX-PRESIDENT VAN BUREN MET LINCOLN, HE CLAIMED HIS "SIDES WERE SORE FROM LAUGHING AT LINCOLN'S STORIES FOR A WEEK THEREAFTER." LINCOLN'S FAVORITE MATERIAL INCLUDED JOKES ABOUT HIS APPEARANCE. AFTER BEING CALLED TWO-FACED, LINCOLN RETORTED, "IF I HAD TWO FACES, WHY WOULD I BE WEARING THIS ONE?"

telegrams for quicker battlefield reporting, and he became a regular at the telegraph office.

AT SIX FEET FOUR (1.9 M), LINCOLN TOWERED OVER MOST PEOPLE. HE ADDED MORE HEIGHT WITH HIS ICONIC "STOVEPIPE" TOP HATS. HE WAS EVEN KNOWN TO KEEP IMPORTANT DOCUMENTS UNDER THERE!

Army to increase in size and called for volunteer soldiers. Normally a president needed permission from Congress for that, but Lincoln felt desperate times called for desperate measures. He was trying to keep a nation together! Next, he blocked all the Confederate ports with Union ships.

HITTING THE BOOKS

The beginning of the war didn't look good for the Union. The first two battles, Fort Sumter and Bull Run in Virginia, were won by the Confederates. Though he served in a volunteer company during the Black Hawk War, Lincoln had never seen battle. As he liked to joke, he had some pretty intense battles with mosquitoes, but that was it.

He wanted to effectively lead his troops, so he immediately began brushing up on military tactics by reading books.

DEMANDER IN CHIEF

For Lincoln, it was victory or else, and he wanted his generals to think the same way. When General McClellan stopped the

Confederates at Antietam in 1862, one of the bloodiest battles in U.S. history, Lincoln eventually relieved him of his post for not more aggressively pursuing the Confederate commander, General Robert E. Lee.

At one point, Lincoln even considered leading his army into battle himself. He found a general he could trust in Ulysses S. Grant. Lincoln liked Grant's relentless nature. Unlike the other generals, Grant chased after various Confederate armies, never letting up and never retreating.

IMPORTANT BILLS

Even though there was a war going on, Lincoln still found time to pass some key legislation. He helped push through the first income tax; the first army draft; the Homestead Act, which gave farmers 160 acres (65 ha) of unsettled territory out West if they stayed for five years; and the National Bank Act. This strengthened the U.S. banking system and created a new currency—the green bills we use today. Greenbacks were paper money that had no gold or silver behind it, just the government's promise that they were good for it.

STICKING IT TO SLAVERY

While Lincoln was personally opposed to slavery, he believed that the primary job of the president was to keep the Union together. As the war dragged on, he came to understand that slavery needed to be abolished once and for all.

When he told his Cabinet he wanted to abolish slavery, they told him to wait until the Union won a great victory so it would look more powerful. Lincoln put his grand idea in the drawer, waiting on his generals to deliver a big win. It took two months.

POWER PLAY

After the Union's big victory at the Battle of Antietam, Lincoln issued the Emancipation Proclamation,

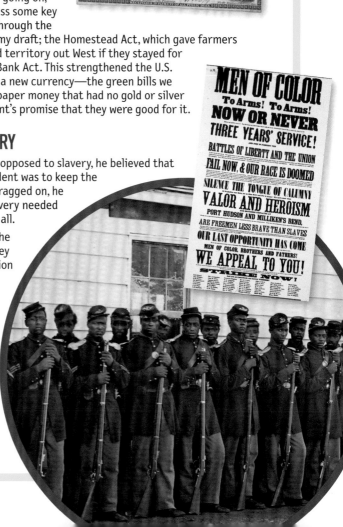

PRESIDENTIAL PREMONITIONS

DAYS BEFORE HE WAS ASSASSINATED, LINCOLN HAD A DREAM WHERE HE WATCHED EVERYONE CRYING OVER HIS BODY IN THE WHITE HOUSE. WEIRDER STILL, LINCOLN SIGNED THE ORDER CREATING THE SECRET SERVICE THE DAY HE WAS KILLED.

which said that if the Confederacy didn't surrender by January 1, 1863, then all slaves in areas under Confederate control would be free. It also authorized the first African-American military units in the Union. Although the proclamation wasn't a law yet, it changed the character of the war—now winning wasn't just about repairing the Union. It was about doing the morally right thing.

MAKING HIS MARK

To make sure slaves would stay free after the war, Lincoln used his powers to push through the 13th Amendment, which formally abolished slavery in the United States. Unfortunately, he wouldn't live to see it included in the Constitution.

THE END

General Lee finally surrendered to General Grant on April 9, 1865, at Appomattox Courthouse, Virginia, ending the war. The Civil War is still the bloodiest war in American history where brother fought brother, and families were torn apart. Roughly 750,000 soldiers died during those four years, and it devastated the young country. But, it officially ended slavery in the U.S. and established the supremacy of federal law over states' rights.

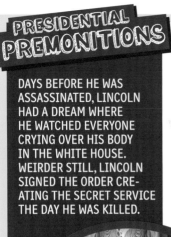

THE BOX AT FORD'S THEATRE IN WASHINGTON, D.C., WHERE PRESIDENT LINCOLN WAS SHOT ON APRIL 14, 1865

TRAGIC FATE

Lincoln wanted to give recently released slaves the right to vote if they were educated or had served in the Union Army. A Confederate supporter, actor, and former militia member named John Wilkes Booth disliked Lincoln's views. Three days after his second inauguration, Lincoln went to see the play *Our American Cousin* at Ford's Theatre in Washington, D.C. Booth slipped into the theater, shot Lincoln in the head, and vaulted onto the stage. Lincoln died nine hours later.

A new uphill battle, Reconstruction, or rebuilding the nation, was left to Lincoln's successor.

ABE OF ALL TRADES

As a young man, Lincoln tried all kinds of jobs, including mailman, blacksmith, store clerk, rail-splitter, and lawyer.

IN THIS TEMPLE
AS IN THE HEARTS OF THE PEOPLE
FOR WHOM HE SAVED THE UNION
THE MEMORY OF ABRAHAM LINCOLN
IS ENSHRINED FOREVER

THE LINCOLN MEMORIAL IN WASHINGTON, D.C., IS AS ROCK-STEADY AS THE MAN HIMSELF.

17TH PRESIDENT
Andrew Johnson
OF THE U.S.A.

★ **TERM** 1865 to 1869
★ **PARTY** Democratic and National Union
★ **NICKNAME** The Tennessee Tailor
★ **CLAIM TO FAME** First president to be impeached
★ **BORN** Raleigh, North Carolina
★ **FIRST LADY** Eliza Johnson (married 1827 to 1875)

"I feel incompetent to perform duties so important and responsible of those which have been so unexpectedly thrown upon me."

Andrew Johnson

PRESIDENTIAL PIZZAZZ Johnson was very handy with a needle and thread. He continued to sew his own clothes—even as president!

Historians tend to agree: Johnson was the wrong man for the job. They accuse him of being a racist Southerner who was never going to give voting rights to African Americans. And now Reconstruction, or rebuilding the Union, was in his hands. Even though the Civil War was over, the hard work was just beginning.

LIONS AND TAILORS AND BEARS, OH MY!

Andrew Johnson made it to the White House without a single day of formal schooling! His family was way too poor for stuff like learning.

Eventually, his mom and stepfather sold the 14-year-old off as an indentured servant to a tailor. That meant Johnson had to work until he was 21 for no wages. Johnson hated it, so he ran away.

Running away before your indentured servant term was up was illegal. So, with a $10 reward for his capture, Johnson stayed on the run for two years.

ANDREW JOHNSON ONCE WOOED A GIRL BY SEWING HER A QUILT!

According to some accounts, he took a blind pony over the mountains, fending off mountain lions and bears, to begin his new life in Tennessee. There, he went from fugitive to mayor to state legislator to governor to senator—despite the fact that he had the spelling skills of an elementary school kid.

BAD OMENS

Andrew Johnson looked up to one major thing—the U.S. Constitution. And it didn't say anything about giving ex-slaves rights. Ultimately, Johnson favored the working man, like himself. He didn't like anyone who made workers' lives harder. In his mind, that included ex-slaves who could take away jobs and land from white Americans. Unfortunately, this belief turned out to be a very bad thing for the newly freed slaves when Johnson became president. He kept vetoing laws that would protect their rights.

UNDER CONSTRUCTION

At first, Johnson had some tough talk for the South, and the Southern aristocrats in particular. After taking office, Johnson required the ex-Confederate states to write new constitutions and abolished slavery. He also demanded that each Southern voter swear loyalty to the U.S. in order to get a pardon. However, most elite Confederates were ineligible for pardons and would therefore not be considered citizens. The only way for them to receive a pardon was to personally apply to Johnson. However, once Johnson's program was in place, he began pardoning important ex-rebels by the thousands! The Republicans in Congress weren't pleased.

SHAKY FOUNDATION

Johnson appointed governors in each defeated state to oversee Reconstruction. Johnson's goal was to have the states write new state constitutions that abolished slavery and to swear loyalty to the Union. He didn't make them add anything else in about rights for African Americans, and in the elections that followed, the ex-Confederate states just reelected all the politicians that got them into a civil war in the first place! These politicians made laws that put life almost exactly back the way it was before the war, including forcing curfews on ex-slaves!

Called Black Codes, these new laws differed from state to state and made freedom close to impossible for the freed slaves. Now, anything from voting, to attending school, to being unemployed could be against the law. And Johnson stood by as it happened. Just because he advocated for the elimination of slavery didn't mean he thought black people should have the same rights as whites.

CRUMBLING APART

To help the newly freed slaves get on their feet, Republicans in Congress passed the Freedmen's Bureau bill. The bureau helped ex-slaves adjust to their new lives by providing education and work opportunities, land, and money for things like food, clothing, and lawyers. Everyone thought Johnson would immediately sign it. Instead, he vetoed it. His reasoning was that freed slaves would not work hard if they had too much help from the government. So Congress passed the Civil Rights Act of 1866, making ex-slaves full citizens entitled to legal protection. Johnson vetoed it, too!

For only the second time in American history, Congress overrode a president's vetoes. Pretty soon it was a political tug-of-war. Every time Congress

PHOTO OF LIBERATED AFRICAN AMERICANS AT CUMBERLAND LANDING, VIRGINIA, 1862

passed a bill, Johnson vetoed it. Then, Congress would override his veto. Finally, Congress decided they'd had enough. This president needed to go.

JUST IMPEACH-Y

The House of Representatives voted to impeach the president for the first time ever. Impeachment happens when a president is found guilty of "treason, bribery, or other high crimes and misdemeanors." Johnson got hit with the charge of committing high crimes and misdemeanors, mainly for violating a law that said he couldn't fire Cabinet officers without getting the Senate to agree to it.

Johnson had to go to the Senate for his impeachment trial, where he was saved from conviction by one measly vote. After all that uproar, Johnson stayed pretty quiet for the rest of his one term. Congress would dominate the remainder of the Reconstruction effort.

SAVED BY THE VOTE!

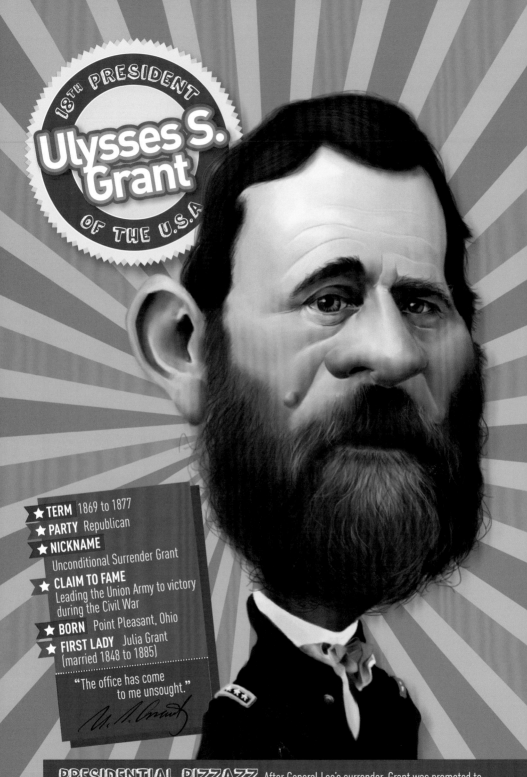

18TH PRESIDENT Ulysses S. Grant OF THE U.S.A.

★ **TERM** 1869 to 1877

★ **PARTY** Republican

★ **NICKNAME**
Unconditional Surrender Grant

★ **CLAIM TO FAME**
Leading the Union Army to victory
during the Civil War

★ **BORN** Point Pleasant, Ohio

★ **FIRST LADY** Julia Grant
(married 1848 to 1885)

"The office has come
to me unsought."

PRESIDENTIAL PIZZAZZ After General Lee's surrender, Grant was promoted to General of the Armies, the first commander since George Washington (who had only received the ▶▶▶

A **circus director** once tried to **unhorse Grant** from a trick pony by **throwing a monkey** at him!

oohhh

Ulysses S. Grant was brave and battle-tested, but as a kid he hated the sight of blood. He was a shy, sensitive boy who the kids nicknamed "useless" at school and only went into the military because his dad made him.

Ulysses's father secretly sought young Ulysses an appointment to the United States Military Academy at West Point where, after he was admitted, he didn't exactly stand out. Out of 39 students, Grant graduated 21st in his class. His true calling, he insisted, was to be a farmer.

THIS SPUD'S A DUD

After graduation, Grant fought in the Mexican-American War. The Army awarded him twice for bravery, but he still never really developed a fondness for fighting. Some years after the war, he left the Army and retired to a farm in Missouri where he built his own cabin log by log. He named it Hardscrabble, because building a log cabin isn't easy, and the end result wasn't exactly pleasing to the eye.

Grant had everything he'd always dreamed of. The problem was he wasn't particularly good at farming. After most of his crop failed, he gave up on the agricultural life.

Luckily, the failed farmer had his soldiering skills to fall back on. When the Civil War broke out in 1861, Grant signed up right away (after all, anything was better than farming potatoes).

WHY HE'S WEIRD!

GRANT LOVED TO FEEL THE WIND IN HIS BEARD. AS PRESIDENT, HE WAS PULLED OVER FOR SPEEDING ON HIS HORSE. HE PROMISED TO SLOW DOWN, BUT LESS THAN 24 HOURS LATER, HE WAS PULLED OVER AGAIN AND ARRESTED.

appointment after his death) to hold that rank.

75

BATTLE OF SHILOH, 1862

RUMPLED BUT RESPECTED

Grant began the Civil War assigned to lead a group of volunteers who were a bit rough around the edges. He used skills learned during the Mexican-American War to whip them into shape in a matter of months. In 1861 and 1862, Grant's troops took control of Confederate-held forts in Kentucky and Tennessee, earning him the nickname "Unconditional Surrender Grant." After that he was assigned major general of the volunteer troops, although you wouldn't know you were looking at a major general by his rumpled appearance.

If he had a motto, it would have been: Never retreat! Never surrender! Brave? Sure. But Grant also refused to retrace his steps. He considered it bad luck. That left him one choice in war: forward. Some critics dubbed him "Grant the Butcher" and said his willingness to plow ahead came from his knowledge that the Union Army far outnumbered the Confederate Army—and that, unlike other generals, he was willing to sacrifice two Union soldiers for every Confederate soldier. Whatever the motivation, it worked. By April 1865, both sides having suffered devastating losses, the Union Army closed in and surrounded Confederate general Robert E. Lee's troops at Appomattox, Virginia, and Lee, Grant's ex–West Point classmate, surrendered to Grant.

RELUCTANT RUN

You'd think becoming president would be the high-light of your life, but for Grant, it was more of a what-the-heck-did-I-get-myself-into moment. Based on the face he showed to the public, he didn't seem particularly interested in politics. In fact, he didn't give any political speeches until years after leaving the White House. The Republicans still unanimously voted him as their candidate, and Grant stomped on his Democratic competition, New York governor Horatio

Seymour. Little did he know that he was about to inadvertently stomp on his own legacy, too.

PRESIDENCY IN PERIL

As it turns out, one of Grant's strengths was also his weakness. He was loyal to his friends and in office, he made the mistake of giving his closest pals jobs in his Cabinet. From the guy who gave him expensive gifts to the guy who helped him buy a house, suddenly it seemed everyone connected to Grant had more power, even if they didn't necessarily understand politics.

By the 1870s, the country was plagued with drama and scandals—with Grant right in the middle. While he himself might have been of good moral character, the same couldn't necessarily be said of his friends. They swindled money from taxpayers, took bribes, and indulged in other shady business practices. Grant wasn't personally involved in any of the scandals, but his reputation took a serious hit anyway. Eventually, the nation encountered an economic slump. In a country still reeling from the Civil War, it made for one rocky road.

H.U.G. ME

IT'S HARD TO LOOK FIERCE AT MILITARY SCHOOL WHEN YOUR INITIALS ARE H.U.G. WELCOME TO GRANT'S WORLD. HIS GIVEN NAME WAS HIRAM ULYSSES GRANT, SO HE STARTED GOING BY ULYSSES H. GRANT. WHEN HE FOUND OUT HE WAS ENROLLED UNDER THE NAME ULYSSES SIMPSON GRANT, SIMPSON BEING HIS MOTHER'S MAIDEN NAME, HE ENDED UP STICKING TO IT.

GLORY, GLORY, GONE!

Aside from the scandals inside his own office, Grant had to deal with serious civil rights issues that plagued the nation. He wanted to help the freed slaves. He signed civil rights legislation into law and, along with support from Congress and three-fourths of the states ratifying it, he signed the 15th Amendment, which granted African-American men the right to vote. He took federal action to break up the Ku Klux Klan, an organization that bolstered white supremacy and intimidated black people. To protect the recently freed slaves, Grant ordered federal troops occupying rebel states to round up and arrest hundreds of Klansmen and put a stop to Klan terrorism.

After two terms, Congress reminded Grant of George Washington's two-term precedent and Grant retired from the presidency. He became a partner at a financial firm, which quickly failed. He spent his later years writing his memoirs.

THE FREEDMEN'S BUREAU—Drawn by A. R. Waud.—[See Page 467.]

19TH PRESIDENT
Rutherford Birchard Hayes
OF THE U.S.A.

★ **TERM** 1877 to 1881
★ **PARTY** Republican
★ **NICKNAME** Rud
★ **CLAIM TO FAME** Winning one of the closest presidential elections in U.S. history
★ **BORN** Delaware, Ohio
★ **FIRST LADY** Lucy Hayes (married 1852 to 1889)

"He serves his party best who serves his country best."

RB Hayes

"RUTHER-FRAUD"

When Hayes's Democratic opponent, Samuel Tilden, was one electoral vote shy of winning the election, men in Hayes's party delayed the announcement long enough for both sides to claim victory, causing mass confusion. There were still 20 disputed electoral votes to be decided. But eventually, a Congressional commission made up of eight Republicans and seven Democrats declared Hayes the winner by, you guessed it, one electoral vote.

The start of Rutherford B. Hayes's presidency was full of promise and hope. He was a man known for his honesty and integrity, and people thought he was the solution to a troubled nation. Instead, his was a contentious four years.

It wasn't completely his fault. Hayes wanted to do awesome things for his country, like clean up the scandals left over from the Grant Administration and heal the still-divided nation. Just to prove he wouldn't allow presidential misdeeds, he promised in advance to serve only one term and make it a good one, but his questionable election doomed him in many voters' eyes.

HAYES HORS D'OEUVRES Hayes himself wrote out his favorite recipe, French pickles, and declared it "excellent." A briny good time!

BIG IDEAS, LITTLE ACTION

When it came to personal philosophy, Hayes was more turtle than hare: slow and steady wins the race. He had lofty ideas that seemed wild for the time, including equal rights for ex-slaves and educational opportunities for all, but he thought big changes wouldn't stick. So he stuck with slow adjustments.

Instead of being remembered for his integrity, Hayes is known for ending Reconstruction in Southern states. He vowed to protect the rights of African Americans, but at the same time believed that the time had come for state governments to assume control over the Reconstruction process. He recalled federal troops that were in place to enforce the protection of recently freed slaves. This move inadvertently left African Americans to fight for their rights alone.

Some historians blame Hayes for these actions, but others point out he did the best he could do for the time—and for serving only one term.

PRESIDENTIAL PRECEDENTS

HAYES WAS THE FIRST PRESIDENT TO:

★ TAKE THE OATH OF OFFICE IN THE WHITE HOUSE— PRIVATELY
★ PUT A TELEPHONE AND TYPEWRITER IN THE WHITE HOUSE
★ CALL HIS WIFE "FIRST LADY" (AND SHE WAS THE FIRST FIRST LADY TO GO TO COLLEGE!)
★ TRAVEL TO THE WEST COAST WHILE IN OFFICE
★ BAN ALCOHOLS FROM THE WHITE HOUSE
★ HOST THE EASTER EGG ROLL ON THE WHITE HOUSE LAWN

As a **colonel,** Rutherford B. Hayes was the only president to be **wounded in the Civil War,** and not just once—**five times!**

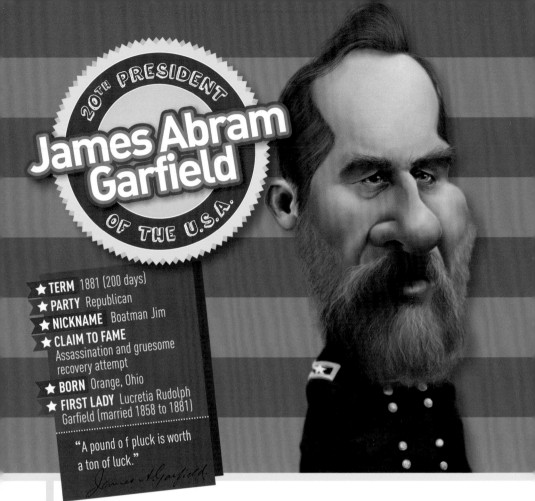

20TH PRESIDENT OF THE U.S.A.

James Abram Garfield

★ **TERM** 1881 (200 days)
★ **PARTY** Republican
★ **NICKNAME** Boatman Jim
★ **CLAIM TO FAME**
Assassination and gruesome recovery attempt
★ **BORN** Orange, Ohio
★ **FIRST LADY** Lucretia Rudolph Garfield (married 1858 to 1881)

"A pound o f pluck is worth a ton of luck."

James A. Garfield

resident Garfield was the second president assassinated in office. Sadly, if it weren't for his doctors, he might have survived.

THE MAN OF MERIT AND THE MADMAN

During his presidency, Garfield tried to pick men for his Cabinet based on their capabilities. Some people didn't like that. They thought they should get a job just because they campaigned for him. One person in particular really took exception to this: Charles Guiteau.

At the time, presidents were not surrounded by armed guards or secret service. Lincoln's assassination was seen as a one-time thing stemming from the stress of the Civil War. Garfield's plans and itinerary were public knowledge, often printed in the paper. Charles Guiteau knew the president's schedule when he went to the Baltimore and Potomac Railroad Station on the morning of July 2, 1881, and shot Garfield twice, once in the back and once in the arm. The president didn't die. Not yet, anyway.

PRESIDENTIAL PIZZAZZ Garfield invited his mom to his inauguration, making him the first president to have his number one fan in attendance.

GARFIELD COULD WRITE ANCIENT GREEK WITH HIS LEFT HAND AND LATIN WITH HIS RIGHT— AT THE SAME TIME!

SICK DAY(S)

For 80 excruciating days, Garfield's doctors poked and prodded his insides looking for the bullet. They tried everything they could think of. Sadly, he succumbed to infection, likely brought on by the doctors' poor hygiene, and he died on September 19, 1881. An autopsy showed the lead bullet encased in a protective cyst—something he could have lived with forever.

GARFIELD THE GREAT

Garfield spent only 200 days in office, but he left a lasting impression. People were so horrified that Garfield had died because some madman wanted a job he didn't deserve that Garfield's vice president, Chester A. Arthur, was able to push through civil service reform. This meant people couldn't get a job because of who they knew—they had to earn it!

WHY HE'S WEIRD!

WHEN GARFIELD WAS 16, HE RAN AWAY FROM HIS LOG CABIN HOME TO WORK ON A CANAL BOAT. SOMEHOW, HE MANAGED TO FALL OVERBOARD 14 TIMES IN HIS FIRST SIX WEEKS OF EMPLOYMENT!

OVAL AWESOME

Garfield thought all men were created equal and should have equal rights as well. That's why he hid a runaway slave and gave ex-slaves, like Frederick Douglass, opportunities in government.

SMART STUFF

Garfield came from a very poor family, but he still found a way to attend the Western Reserve Eclectic Institute in Ohio—by becoming a janitor. He later graduated with honors from Williams College. He was so smart, the institute appointed him president of the school when he was only 26!

21ST PRESIDENT
Chester Alan Arthur
OF THE U.S.A.

- ★ **TERM** 1881 to 1885
- ★ **PARTY** Republican
- ★ **NICKNAME** The Gentleman Boss
- ★ **CLAIM TO FAME**
  Pendleton Civil Service Act
- ★ **BORN** Fairfield, Vermont
- ★ **SPOUSE** Ellen Arthur
  (married 1859 to 1880; died the year
  before he became president)

"Men may die, but the fabrics
of free institutions
remains unshaken."

Chester A. Arthur

PRESIDENTIAL PIZZAZZ Chester A. Arthur was the first president to have a personal valet, or male attendant. He also supposedly owned eighty extravagant pairs of pants and ▶▶▶

PRESIDENT "NIGHT-OWL" ARTHUR WOULD SOMETIMES WALK THE WHITE HOUSE GROUNDS UNTIL THREE IN THE MORNING AND SNOOZE TILL NOON.

hoot

Chester A. Arthur cruised into the presidency by chance after James Garfield's assassination. Some historians say he was charmed in this respect, happening into positions of power. After all, he got the job of vice president because his big-time New York friends were very influential in politics and New York was an important state in the presidential election. Of course, all his friends thought he'd return the favor as president. They were wrong.

President Arthur started making his buddies suspicious when he refused to give them government jobs. He set out to reform the civil service system, especially on the heels of Garfield's death. But many Republicans were disenchanted with Arthur's limited reforms, and the party refused to nominate him for another term.

GETTING GUMPTION

During his time in office, Arthur organized the International Meridian Conference, which set up today's time zones. He also signed the Pendleton Civil Service Act, ousting the spoils system that, among other things, meant that nonpolitical jobs were now given based upon merit, not who you knew. But his legislation wasn't always what was best for the country or its people. Arthur also signed into law the Chinese Exclusion Act, which prevented all Chinese people from coming to the United States. It wasn't until 1965 that large-scale Chinese immigration to the U.S. was allowed to resume.

Arthur's presidency wasn't quite as fancy as his carefully coiffed muttonchops, but he got the ball rolling by beginning to tackle corruption in Washington.

WHY HE'S WEIRD!

PRESIDENT ARTHUR LIKED NICE THINGS. ONCE HE GOT TO THE WHITE HOUSE, HE DECIDED TO HAVE A GARAGE SALE. HE SOLD EVERYTHING FROM HISTORICAL HATS TO PAST PRESIDENTS' PANTS. THEN HE FOUND THE MOST EXPENSIVE INTERIOR DECORATOR IN THE COUNTRY TO SPRUCE UP THE PLACE: LOUIS C. TIFFANY, A NAME SYNONYMOUS WITH A LUXURY BRAND THAT'S STILL AROUND TODAY.

GARAGE SALE
1600 Pennsylvania Ave.

wore fur-trimmed coats. Talk about a leader of luxury!

22ND & 24TH PRESIDENT
Grover Cleveland
OF THE U.S.A.

★ **TERM** 1885 to 1889 and 1893 to 1897
★ **PARTY** Democrat
★ **NICKNAME** Uncle Jumbo
★ **CLAIM TO FAME** Enforcing the Monroe Doctrine, dedicating the Statue of Liberty
★ **BORN** Caldwell, New Jersey
★ **FIRST LADY** Frances Folsom Cleveland (married 1886 to 1908)

" ... though the people support the Government, the Government should not support the people."

As president, Grover Cleveland thought the government did too much. He felt it was his job to watchdog the government, so he vetoed more than two times the number of bills than all the previous presidents combined! After one term, he lost reelection to Benjamin Harrison. But he wasn't finished yet.

Cleveland is the only president to serve two nonconsecutive (not back-to-back) terms.

GROVER THE GOOD Before getting into politics, Cleveland was a sheriff!

HARD LINE

During his first term, Cleveland signed the controversial Dawes Act, which was an attempt to force Native Americans to assimilate (fit into) white American society. Historians agree that the act was devastating for Native Americans. It was finally abolished in 1934 under Franklin D. Roosevelt.

He also sought to reduce the expenses of the government. He famously vetoed a bill that was going to distribute grain to farmers who were suffering during the bad economy, and vetoed a bunch of bills that would give veterans money, because he thought they were fraudulent. He believed the American people might start relying on the government for handouts, a policy that received mixed reviews. Many people also felt his attempts to lower protective tariffs (taxes) threatened industrial jobs. He lost reelection to Harrison.

UNDONE AND JUST BEGUN

Cleveland nabbed the top job four years later. He spent his second term undoing the things that President Harrison had done, which included temporarily stopping the annexation (taking over) of Hawaii. According to Cleveland, America needed to keep its nose in its own business, and stay out of world affairs that might mean international commitments.

HARD LABOR

During his second term, the Pullman Strike happened. In response to severely cut wages and facing starvation, thousands of workers at the Pullman Railroad Company (and eventually other railroad companies) walked off the job. Then the workers got violent with a U.S. mail train and Cleveland wasn't pleased. He sent federal troops into Chicago to ensure trains kept moving, which angered the workers even more and led to more violence. Eventually, the strike lost momentum and the railroad companies reopened, but the workers were still peeved. To appease the American labor force, Cleveland created a federal holiday for them—Labor Day.

The bad economy and strike controversies kept his party from renominating him for a third term.

WHY HE'S WEIRD!

AT AGE 49, PRESIDENT CLEVELAND WAS READY TO SETTLE DOWN. HE BECAME THE FIRST SITTING PRESIDENT TO MARRY INSIDE THE WHITE HOUSE WHEN HE SAID "I DO" TO 21-YEAR-OLD FRANCES FOLSOM. THIS MADE HER THE YOUNGEST FIRST LADY EVER AND AN INSTANT HIT WITH THE PUBLIC.

GO AWAY

Cleveland wanted America to stay out of world affairs, but he also wanted the world to stay out of the Americas. Cleveland told Britain to back away from Venezuela, in South America—or else.

23RD PRESIDENT
Benjamin Harrison
OF THE U.S.A.

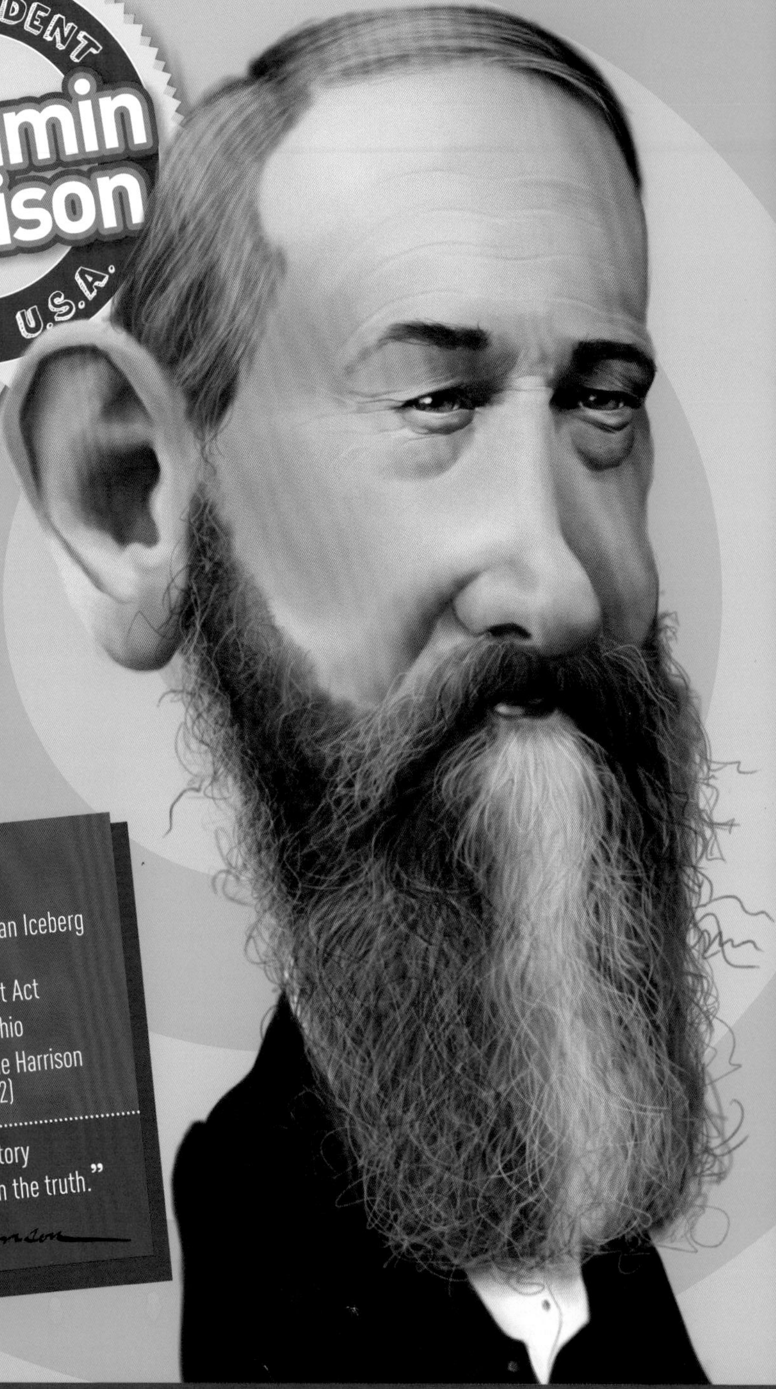

- **TERM** 1889 to 1893
- **PARTY** Republican
- **NICKNAME** The Human Iceberg
- **CLAIM TO FAME** The Sherman Antitrust Act
- **BORN** North Bend, Ohio
- **FIRST LADY** Caroline Harrison (married 1853 to 1892)

"... the bud of victory is always in the truth."

Benj Harrison

PRESIDENTIAL PIZZAZZ Harrison's family brought back dancing to the White House after the long dance drought started by the Polks!

Benjamin Harrison was not exactly a people person. He could deliver a dynamic speech, but one-on-one he came off a bit frigid. Many people, including his own staff, referred to him as the "Human Iceberg." But his party held a majority in both houses of Congress, and they wanted the same things, like money for veterans and their families. Since Harrison fought for the North during the Civil War, he wanted African Americans to have the right to vote, too. Most Southern states had figured out ways to continue to ban them from voting even after the 15th Amendment passed. This is where Congress differed. While the Senate shot his bill down, he still tried to help by naming African Americans to government posts. He also signed what was at the time the most powerful piece of antimonopoly legislation ever passed by Congress, the Sherman Antitrust Act of 1890, which tried to force big business to treat the American public with more fairness.

BENJAMIN HARRISON WAS THE **FIRST** PRESIDENT TO HAVE HIS **VOICE** RECORDED!

BILLION-DOLLAR MAN

Under Harrison, Congress spent a billion dollars during peacetime. They used it to strengthen the Navy with 19 new ships, and Harrison began Hawaii's annexation (establishing it as a territory). Six new states were brought into the Union during Harrison's presidency, and the first conference between North and South American countries occurred. Harrison had a powerful imperial vision and he literally let his pride fly by urging the country to hoist the Stars and Stripes over public buildings and schools.

Unfortunately for his reelection bid, a serious drought mixed with sky-high taxes that increased food prices brought the most serious depression (economic downturn) to date. So people voted his nemesis, Grover Cleveland, back into office (see page 85).

WHY HE'S WEIRD

Harrison was the first president to have electricity installed in the White House, but unfortunately he was so afraid of getting electrocuted that he never touched the light switches!

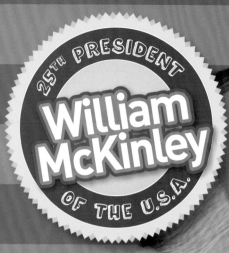

25TH PRESIDENT
William McKinley
OF THE U.S.A.

- ★ **TERM** 1897 to 1901
- ★ **PARTY** Republican
- ★ **NICKNAME** Napoleon of Protection
- ★ **CLAIM TO FAME** Declaring war on Spain
- ★ **BORN** Niles, Ohio
- ★ **FIRST LADY** Ida Saxton McKinley (married 1871 to 1901)

"War should never be entered upon until every agency of peace has failed."

William McKinley

PRESIDENTIAL PIZZAZZ William McKinley spent a lot of his presidential paycheck on nice clothing for himself and his wife, Ida, changing up to four times a day. When ▶▶▶

McKinley was a charmer who could win over the grumpiest senator. He was well-liked and admired. Sadly, his presidency was cut short a year into his second term when he was assassinated by a man who distrusted the government in general.

SORROWS WITH SPAIN

American politicians didn't like the way Spain was running things in their Cuban colony. The Cuban people wanted liberty, and journalists at the time reported—not always accurately—on poor conditions, including work camps, disease, and death. There were also many Americans who wanted to claim Cuba as a U.S. territory, especially an American businessman who had millions of dollars invested in Cuban sugar. The U.S. was hungry for war, but not McKinley. He tried to work things out peacefully with Spain—until he found out the Spanish ambassador was badmouthing him behind his back.

The American people thought his pride (and theirs) was on the line. Then the American battleship, the U.S.S. *Maine*, blew up in Cuba's port, killing 266 men. It was an engine failure, but many assumed it was Spanish sabotage. McKinley finally asked Congress to declare war.

WHY HE'S WEIRD!

AS A KID, WILLIAM MCKINLEY HAD THE IMPORTANT JOB OF FAMILY COW HERDER. HE HERDED THE CATTLE TO AND FROM THE PASTURE, OFTEN BAREFOOT. EVEN SNOW ON THE GROUND DIDN'T STOP HIM! THE NINE-YEAR-OLD LOVED TO DIG HIS TOES INTO THE WARM EARTH WHERE THE COWS HAD POOPED, CALLING IT "PURE LUXURY."

one vest became wrinkled, he'd simply pull out the next freshly pressed one!

DETECTIVE MCKINLEY

McKinley really liked being liked, so whenever he met someone new, he was like a detective on a case: constantly questioning what they thought about his policies. A senator once said that McKinley kept his ear so close to the ground that it was probably full of grasshoppers!

EXPANDING EMPIRE

The fighting in the Spanish-American War lasted less than four months and fewer than 400 Americans died in battle. In the Spanish surrender, America received the Philippines, Puerto Rico, and Guam as new territories. McKinley also pushed through the annexation of Hawaii that had plagued the past two presidents. Together, they made up America's first overseas colonies.

STATE OF CONFUSION

In addition to a lesson in foreign affairs, McKinley also got one in geography. When word came from his naval commander in the Pacific Ocean, Admiral George Dewey, that he'd won a battle in Manila Bay, McKinley's secretary found him leafing through a children's textbook to find a map of the islands while sheepishly saying, "It is evident that I must learn a great deal of geography in this war."

PROPPING THE DOOR

For McKinley's second act, he didn't have time to campaign. He had a lot on his plate with more international disputes. This time, it meant war with the Philippines, which didn't like being handed off between countries. America also got involved in a skirmish with China.

With his Open Door policy, McKinley said all countries could trade with China equally, and no one was allowed to conquer them. The Boxers, a nationalist Chinese group, fought to force all foreigners out, so McKinley sent in soldiers to keep China open.

PRESIDENT MCKINLEY HAD A **PARROT** NAMED WASHINGTON POST THAT WHISTLED "YANKEE DOODLE" **DUETS** WITH HIM!

tweet!

The trouble abroad didn't affect McKinley's reelection bid, though. Thanks to his successes, most Americans thought the president was a winner. The Republican Party picked war hero Theodore Roosevelt as his running mate even though the two were as different as puppies and porcupines.

POWER PLAY

McKinley was considered a successful president—but even good guys aren't liked by everyone. Sadly, when McKinley was shaking hands and kissing babies in Buffalo, New York, he met one man who hated the government.

Leon Czolgosz decided the best way to eliminate the power of the government was to eliminate the person at the top. He hid a gun in a handkerchief wrapped around his hand. Instead of shaking McKinley's, he pulled the trigger.

The president died eight days later.

TOUCHING TRIBUTE

MCKINLEY WAS KNOWN FOR THE TINY RED CARNATION FLOWER HE ALWAYS KEPT IN HIS LAPEL. HE CONSIDERED IT HIS GOOD LUCK CHARM. JUST MINUTES BEFORE HE WAS SHOT, MCKINLEY SUPPOSEDLY TOOK IT OFF AND PRESENTED HIS CHARM TO A YOUNG GIRL. THREE YEARS LATER, HIS HOME STATE OF OHIO ADOPTED THE RED CARNATION AS ITS STATE FLOWER.

PRESIDENT MCKINLEY PHOTOGRAPHED FROM THE BACK OF A TRAIN IN 1900

PRESIDENTIAL PROWESS

McKinley had a photographic memory. As president, he met hundreds of people a day and could remember their names a month later!

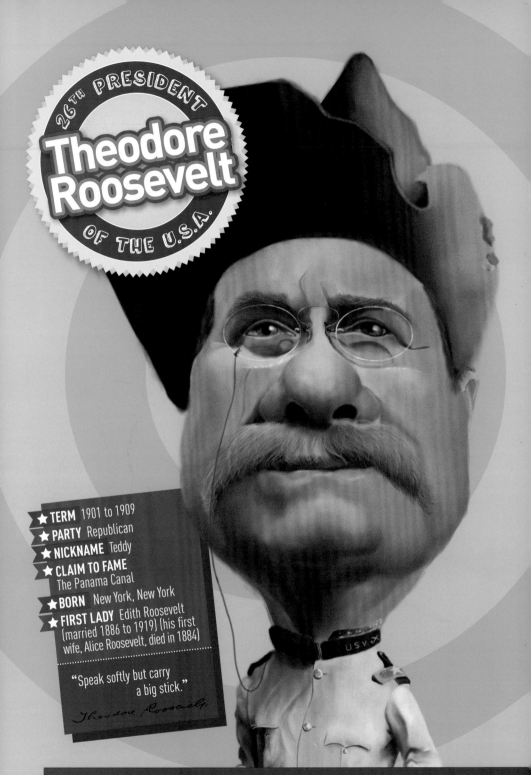

26TH PRESIDENT
Theodore Roosevelt
OF THE U.S.A.

★ **TERM** 1901 to 1909
★ **PARTY** Republican
★ **NICKNAME** Teddy
★ **CLAIM TO FAME**
The Panama Canal
★ **BORN** New York, New York
★ **FIRST LADY** Edith Roosevelt
(married 1886 to 1919) (his first
wife, Alice Roosevelt, died in 1884)

"Speak softly but carry
a big stick."

Theodore Roosevelt

PRESIDENTIAL PIZZAZZ Roosevelt led diplomats on hiking expeditions, set up target practice with his revolver, chopped down trees, and skinny-dipped in the Potomac River.

Theodore Roosevelt is a bit like a cartoon superhero come to life. He gave 110 percent to everything he did. Like during the Spanish-American War, when he resigned from his government job to organize the first volunteer cavalry (horseback soldiers called the Rough Riders), mounted up, and led the charge up San Juan Hill in Cuba to help achieve victory. One thing's for sure: Roosevelt had a larger-than-life personality, and he left quite a mark on America and the presidency.

"CRAZY COWBOY"

When Teddy was sworn in only six months into McKinley's four-year term (due to McKinley's assassination), the new commander in chief unnerved some people with his love of boxing, bear hunting, and backpacking. He was the youngest president ever at age 42 and by some accounts had more energy than a sugared-up puppy. Would he get the country into war? Maybe he'd make foreign diplomats go three rounds in the ring to settle their issues! This Rough Rider was a wild card!

BULLY FOR YOU!

For all his spark and charisma, it turns out Roosevelt liked to talk more than he liked to listen. According to contemporaries, he played favorites, enjoyed being flattered, and was impulsive. He'd call men in Congress "crooks" and "fools," which went over about as well as you can imagine. But angering Congress didn't seem to worry Teddy; he did what he wanted. If something bored him, like tariffs, his policy was generally to ignore the issue. But he fascinated the American public, and they loved him.

Introducing: the bully pulpit.

Teddy figured the presidency was the best platform in the world, so he used it to advocate for things he thought were important, like a decent quality of living. He called his policies a "Square Deal" for the American people, emphasizing conservation of natural resources, control of big corporations, and consumer protection.

TEDDY ROOSEVELT WENT **BLIND** IN HIS LEFT **EYE** WHEN HE WAS INJURED IN A **BOXING MATCH** WHILE HE WAS **PRESIDENT.**

ON TOP OF THE WORLD

Teddy enjoyed the great outdoors so much, he was out there every chance he had. In fact, he was hiking the Adirondack Mountains when he found out he was president!

TEDDY THE TRUSTBUSTER

Teddy didn't just go on the defense for the little guys—he also attacked big businesses, called trusts. One trust, the Northern Securities Company, was a bunch of big railroad companies that banded together to form one massive company. They ruled the rails, meaning they could control the prices, and Teddy thought that was an unfair deal. He said they violated the Sherman Antitrust law, and the Supreme Court agreed. The trust was busted, and Teddy earned the nickname "Trustbuster."

PRESIDENTIAL PRECEDENTS

ROOSEVELT WAS THE FIRST PRESIDENT TO:
★ FLY IN AN AIRPLANE
★ HAVE THE FIRST GOVERNMENT-OWNED CAR
★ DIVE IN A SUBMARINE
★ TRAVEL OUTSIDE THE U.S. WHILE PRESIDENT (TO PANAMA)
★ OFFICIALLY LABEL THE WHITE HOUSE
★ INVITE AN AFRICAN AMERICAN (BOOKER T. WASHINGTON) TO DINNER AT THE WHITE HOUSE
★ WIN THE NOBEL PEACE PRIZE (FIRST AMERICAN TO WIN, TOO)
★ RECEIVE A CONGRESSIONAL MEDAL OF HONOR (IN 2001)

THE FIGHT AGAINST FOUL FOOD

Teddy went after the food industry next. Newspapers were still the main form of communication in the country, and a new breed of journalist—Teddy called them muckrakers—were digging up some foul atrocities happening in government and business. Roosevelt did not like these pot-stirrers, but he could not ignore the evidence they brought to light. After reading a book by Upton Sinclair called *The Jungle* about the darker side of industrial capitalism, which also exposed some horrifying practices in the meatpacking industry, Roosevelt began to champion laws for regulation on food production.

It wasn't right to him that regular people got sick and died from eating rattail sausage links or apples dyed red with poisonous chemicals. In 1906, Roosevelt signed the Meat Inspection Act and the Pure Food and Drug Act. Now the federal government could sniff out any funny business.

BIG-STICK POLITICS

As much as Teddy enjoyed policing policies at home, he enjoyed flexing his muscles abroad, too. To Teddy, war should be avoided, but showing off America's power and resources would go a long way in keeping the peace.

He started by adding the Roosevelt Corollary to the Monroe Doctrine. It stated that the U.S. would step in if European powers got involved in affairs of the Americas, and that if there was going to be any fighting between Central or South American countries or internal turmoil in those nations, the U.S. reserved the right to intervene.

To make sure everyone knew he was dead serious about the growth of the U.S. as a world power, Roosevelt sent 16 white warships to sail around the world as part of a "peacekeeping mission."

PRESIDENTIAL PIZZAZZ

THEODORE ROOSEVELT MAY HAVE GROWN UP A RICH CITY KID, BUT THAT DIDN'T MEAN HE WAS AFRAID TO GET HIS HANDS DIRTY. HE SPENT TWO YEARS ON A RANCH, RIDING HORSES, DRIVING CATTLE, AND EVEN CATCHING SOME OUTLAWS WHO STOLE HIS BOAT.

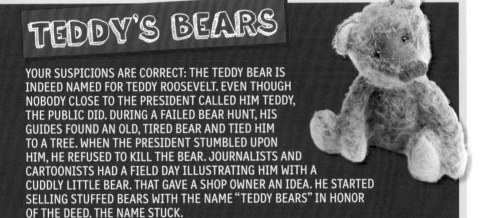

TEDDY'S BEARS

YOUR SUSPICIONS ARE CORRECT: THE TEDDY BEAR IS INDEED NAMED FOR TEDDY ROOSEVELT. EVEN THOUGH NOBODY CLOSE TO THE PRESIDENT CALLED HIM TEDDY, THE PUBLIC DID. DURING A FAILED BEAR HUNT, HIS GUIDES FOUND AN OLD, TIRED BEAR AND TIED HIM TO A TREE. WHEN THE PRESIDENT STUMBLED UPON HIM, HE REFUSED TO KILL THE BEAR. JOURNALISTS AND CARTOONISTS HAD A FIELD DAY ILLUSTRATING HIM WITH A CUDDLY LITTLE BEAR. THAT GAVE A SHOP OWNER AN IDEA. HE STARTED SELLING STUFFED BEARS WITH THE NAME "TEDDY BEARS" IN HONOR OF THE DEED. THE NAME STUCK.

HATS OFF TO PANAMA

To illustrate U.S. power in the Americas, U.S. construction on the Panama Canal finally got under way. Instead of having to sail all the way around South America to get to the Pacific Ocean, it would be faster to cut in between the narrow strip of land between North and South America. That happened to be in present-day Panama, which was at the time a Colombian territory.

AS A ROUGH RIDER CHARGING INTO BATTLE WITH HIS COWBOYS OR AS A FAMILY MAN WITH HIS SIX KIDS, ROOSEVELT ALWAYS ROLLED WITH A SQUAD. ROOSEVELT HAD THE ENTIRE WEST WING BUILT TO HOUSE HIS BEASTLY CREW, WHICH INCLUDED A BEAR, DOGS, TWO CATS, FIVE GUINEA PIGS, A LIZARD, TWO PARROTS, A BLUE MACAW, A HEN, A ONE-LEGGED ROOSTER, A BADGER, A RABBIT, A HYENA, AND TOO MANY SNAKES TO COUNT. HIS KIDS TOOK TO ALL THAT EXTRA SPACE A LITTLE TOO ENTHUSIASTICALLY. THEY BROUGHT THEIR PONY, ALGONQUIN, ON THE ELEVATOR, DROPPED WATER BALLOONS ON GUARDS' HEADS, AND TRIED TO SCARE GOVERNMENT OFFICIALS WITH THEIR FOUR-FOOT (1.2-M) KING SNAKE.

After negotiations with Colombia for the land fell through, the U.S. resorted to new measures by actively and successfully supporting a movement for Panamanian independence. Some historians consider this a "closed-door" deal, meaning the public was not privy to the details, but in the end Teddy secured the rights to 10 miles (16 km) of that strip and personally traveled there to watch men dig it up. When it was finished in 1914, the constructed canal cut the distance between New York and San Francisco by 8,000 miles (12,875 km)!

ROUGH RIDER

Teddy Roosevelt loved to talk, and nothing could stop him from making his point. Not even a bullet. In 1912, while running for the presidency again, Roosevelt took a bullet to the chest and barely noticed, except for the blood. He showed the crowd, saying, "Friends, I shall ask you to be as quiet as possible. I don't know whether you fully understand that I have just been shot; but it takes more than that to kill a Bull Moose." He finished his speech and allowed himself to be taken to the hospital—an hour later.

roar

EARLY IN HIS PRESIDENCY, ROOSEVELT DECIDED HE WANTED TO KEEP NATURE AROUND. ON A 1903 TRIP TO IDAHO, HE SAID, "WE MUST HANDLE THE WATER, THE WOODS, THE GRASSES, SO THAT WE WILL HAND THEM ON TO OUR CHILDREN AND CHILDREN'S CHILDREN IN BETTER AND NOT WORSE SHAPE THAN WE GOT THEM."

NATIONAL PARKS ADDED BY TEDDY: 5

NATIONAL PARKS TODAY: 59
(TOTAL PROTECTED AREAS IN THE NATIONAL PARK SYSTEM: 410)

LARGE AND IN CHARGE

When he got elected in 1904, Teddy promised he wouldn't run again, even though he technically could have. Instead, he used his celebrity-like popularity to put his favorite guy, William Howard Taft, in office after him.

While he was in charge, Teddy did things presidents before him never dreamed of doing, like issuing over a thousand executive orders. He made the position of president more important than Congress for the first time in decades. That's why some historians refer to him as the first modern president.

ILL-POWER

Part of Roosevelt's larger-than-life persona was due to a childhood plagued by illness. Doctors told his parents he might not live to see his fourth birthday. Instead of sitting around feeling sorry for himself, young Theodore did the opposite: He became extremely athletic. By taking up any activity that made him sweat, the frail, nearsighted boy turned himself into a rugged outdoorsman. And he still found time to read a book a day and write some 45 of his own!

27TH PRESIDENT
William Howard Taft
OF THE U.S.A.

★ **TERM** 1909 to 1913

★ **PARTY** Republican

★ **NICKNAME** Big Bill

★ **CLAIM TO FAME** Being the only president to later serve on the Supreme Court as the Chief Justice

★ **BORN** Cincinnati, Ohio

★ **FIRST LADY** Helen Taft (married 1886 to 1930)

" I don't remember that I was ever president. "

PRESIDENTIAL PRECEDENT Taft added his own addition to Theodore Roosevelt's West Wing. He built the fabled Oval Office over an old tennis court and painted it grass green.

Taft had been Theodore Roosevelt's protégé. The super-popular Roosevelt backed him for the top job, and that was good enough for a majority of Americans. The newspapers even claimed his last name stood for: Take Advice From Theodore. But then Roosevelt went on a yearlong hunting safari, and Taft had the White House to himself.

TRUSTBUSTER

Historians say Taft didn't like being president, but one thing he did seem to enjoy, even more so than Teddy, was busting trusts. Taft busted double the number of trusts that Roosevelt had in half the time, including giant sugar, oil, and tobacco companies that had become monopolies. Unfortunately for their relationship, that included going after trusts Roosevelt *didn't* want busted, like one he really liked: U.S. Steel. Roosevelt said Taft couldn't tell the difference between good and bad big business.

WHY HE'S WEIRD!

AMERICANS ATE SOME PRETTY WEIRD STUFF BACK IN 1900, INCLUDING POSSUM. AT AN ATLANTA, GEORGIA, BANQUET, THE PRESIDENT ATE A LARGE POSSUM, AND THEN WAS PRESENTED WITH A SMALL TOY—THE BILLY POSSUM. THIS MONEYMAKING SCHEME WAS MEANT TO REPLICATE THE SMASHING SUCCESS OF TEDDY BEARS, BUT THE STUFFED POSSUMS FELL A BIT FLAT.

'POSSUM BILLY'

TAFT LOVED BASEBALL SO MUCH HE THREW OUT THE FIRST "FIRST PITCH" ON OPENING DAY FOR THE WASHINGTON SENATORS IN 1910, STARTING A LONG-RUNNING TRADITION!

A PARTY DIVIDED

After four years of Teddy believing that Taft had not followed his advice closely enough, the old Rough Rider called him a traitor (among other not-nice things), and took over the Progressive Party to run against Taft in 1912. Teddy split the Republican votes, which allowed Woodrow Wilson, a Democrat, to pounce on the White House.

ORDER IN THE COURT!

After his presidency, all the scholarly Taft wanted was to serve on the Supreme Court. He finally got his wish when President Harding named him Chief Justice in 1921. Taft was thrilled. He became the only person to have served as head of two branches of the U.S. government—the executive and the judicial—and he swore in two presidents, Coolidge and Hoover.

Woodrow Wilson

OF THE U.S.A.

★ **TERM** 1913 to 1921
★ **PARTY** Democrat
★ **NICKNAME** The Schoolmaster
★ **CLAIM TO FAME** Ending World War I
★ **BORN** Staunton, Virginia
★ **FIRST LADY**
Ellen Wilson (married 1885 to 1914),
Edith Wilson (married 1915 to 1924)

"The Constitution was not made to fit us like a straitjacket."

Woodrow Wilson

OVAL AWESOME Wilson did his part for the war effort. To save money, his wife Edith brought in sheep to munch on the White House lawn. They really cut down landscaping ▶▶▶

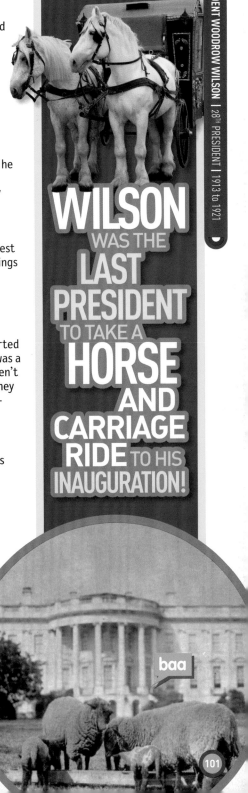

As the only president to have earned a Ph.D., Wilson was smart, and he wanted great things for America. But his doctorate was in history and political science, not diplomacy. At Princeton University, when reminded that there were two sides to every argument, he responded, "Yes. A right side and a wrong side."

CHAMPION FOR CHANGE

Wilson wanted to reform America financially, and he called his grand plan New Freedom. To do this, he broke tradition by coming to Congress personally and explaining his idea on lowering tariffs. High tariffs raised the prices on imported goods, and Wilson thought this hurt regular folks by making them pay outrageous prices. He wanted the poorest people to have the same opportunities to buy things as the rich. It worked, and Congress passed the Revenue Act of 1913.

BANKING ON THE BANK

The whole basis of our banking system today started under Wilson. Before him, the monetary system was a free-for-all, and frequent economic "panics" weren't exactly comforting to the American people. So they demanded reform. Wilson proposed more government control over banks.

The Federal Reserve Act of 1913 made one national, central bank that could adjust certain things according to what the market needed. This helped smooth the flow of the U.S. economy.

WILSON WAS THE LAST PRESIDENT TO TAKE A HORSE AND CARRIAGE RIDE TO HIS INAUGURATION!

NO VETO

Congress didn't always listen to Wilson. They overrode his veto on the Volstead Act. This act enforced Prohibition in the United States, which meant selling alcohol was off-limits!

baa

costs, and the wool was auctioned off to raise money for the Red Cross!

CHILD WORKERS AT THE LOUISIANA OYSTER CANNERY IN 1911

CHAMPION OF THE PEOPLE

Next, Wilson tackled labor. In the days when workers didn't have many rights in the workplace, and unreasonably long hours were commonplace, Wilson demanded a standard eight-hour workday for railroad workers and no more child labor. This helped pave the way for all types of workers to get more rights.

He also signed the Federal Trade Commission Act, which allowed the government to investigate bad business practices. (For example, no more "cure-all" tonics that claimed to cure cancer, warts, and measles for the low, low price of an entire paycheck!)

BACKWARD POLICIES

For Wilson, the right to vote for women wasn't at the top of his list, and he jailed those bold enough to protest on the White House lawn. He grudgingly supported a constitutional amendment guaranteeing women the vote only when it seemed politically necessary.

Wilson was also not very progressive when it came to race. He thought it was better if African Americans stayed out of federal jobs. For the first time since the Civil War, he segregated the government, and during this time, the KKK, a white supremacy group, reemerged.

OVAL AWFUL

Movie lover Wilson screened the first movie inside the White House, *The Birth of a Nation*. Unfortunately, the controversial film was about two families during and after the Civil War, and it romanticized the white South and the KKK. The movie also quoted Wilson, and he liked that. Three years later, Wilson backtracked and wrote in a letter, "I have always felt that this was a very unfortunate production, and I wish most sincerely that its production might have been avoided."

D.W. GRIFFITH'S MIGHTY SPECTACLE
THE BIRTH OF A NATION
FOUNDED ON THOMAS DIXON'S THE CLANSMAN

NEUTRAL NATION

Wilson had no interest in getting the U.S. involved in another war. As a child in the South, he'd lived through the Civil War and knew firsthand the atrocities of battle. But tensions were high between European nations as the balance of power was shifting and countries were forming alliances. Then, in 1914, Archduke Franz Ferdinand, heir to the Austro-Hungarian Empire, was assassinated by a Serbian nationalist. This was the spark that ignited World War I. Austria-Hungary, Germany, Bulgaria, and the Ottoman Empire (the Central Powers) were pitted against Serbia's network of allies: Russia, France, Great Britain, Italy, and Japan.

Back in the U.S., news from the European trenches wasn't good: In one day of fighting alone, German machine guns killed 27,000 French soldiers. And that was just a fraction of the eventual death toll. Wilson promised peace and held regular press conferences to talk the public into staying neutral. He even won reelection on the slogan "He kept us out of war." That lasted a month after his second inauguration.

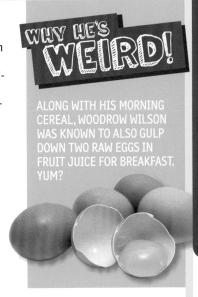

WHY HE'S WEIRD!

ALONG WITH HIS MORNING CEREAL, WOODROW WILSON WAS KNOWN TO ALSO GULP DOWN TWO RAW EGGS IN FRUIT JUICE FOR BREAKFAST. YUM?

CROSSING THE LINE

German U-boat submarines attacked anything that floated, including neutral passenger ships. In May 1915, the British ocean liner the *Lusitania* was carrying 128 Americans when the Germans torpedoed it. Wilson gave a stern warning: Don't do it again, or else. In March 1916, the Germans badly damaged a British passenger ferry, the *Sussex*. Again, Wilson told them to watch it.

The final straw came in 1917 via the Zimmermann telegram, in which the German foreign minister Arthur Zimmermann told Mexico that, if Mexico attacked the U.S., Mexico could reclaim the territory the U.S. had taken after the Mexican-American War in the 1840s. Big mistake. Wilson went to Congress and the U.S. declared war.

THE (NOT SO) GREAT WAR

Once Wilson went in, he went *all* in. He controlled all aspects of wartime life, including the draft (required military duty), freedom of speech, and how much coal everyone received. He also introduced the Espionage Act and the Sedition Act. It didn't matter who you were, if you were caught badmouthing the war or urging people to dodge the draft, you could be arrested, put on trial, and sent to prison.

His wartime measures led to hundreds of thousands of American troops pouring into Europe. Germany surrendered in November 1918, but not before the world suffered 38 million casualties.

MR. AMERICA

After the war, Wilson wanted a "just and secure peace," not just a shake-up of power. He sailed off to Paris to help with peace talks himself. It was the first time a sitting president traveled to Europe.

There, Wilson argued for his Fourteen Points plan. It presented terms in which Germany wouldn't have to say they started the war, nations would band together to form the League of Nations, and hopefully world peace would reign. Wilson's dream was to move on together.

Not everyone loved it. France and Britain gutted part of his plan. But they agreed on the League of Nations, and Wilson signed the Treaty of Versailles. They made Germany pay the equivalent of U.S. $33 billion in reparations (or, "we're sorry" money), reduce their army, and accept full responsibility for the start of the war. These conditions crippled and embarrassed Germany, and they helped set the stage for Adolf Hitler's rise to power only a few years later.

STATE OF DISUNION

Back home in the U.S., many Americans didn't accept the Fourteen Points plan that their own president presented, either! Republicans were worried the League of Nations would drag the U.S. into another war. Wilson ran himself ragged trying to drum up support for it all across America, and suffered a series of debilitating strokes. For two years afterward, his wife Edith assisted in running the executive branch.

Historians say Wilson refused to compromise on so much as a comma of his Fourteen Points. While the Treaty of Paris failed to pass Congress—twice—Wilson did receive a Nobel Peace Prize for trying.

PRESIDENTIAL SOUND BITE

Wilson knew if the League of Nations failed, there would never be world peace. He even said, "I can predict with absolute certainty that within another generation there will be another world war." He was right. World War II was less than 20 years away.

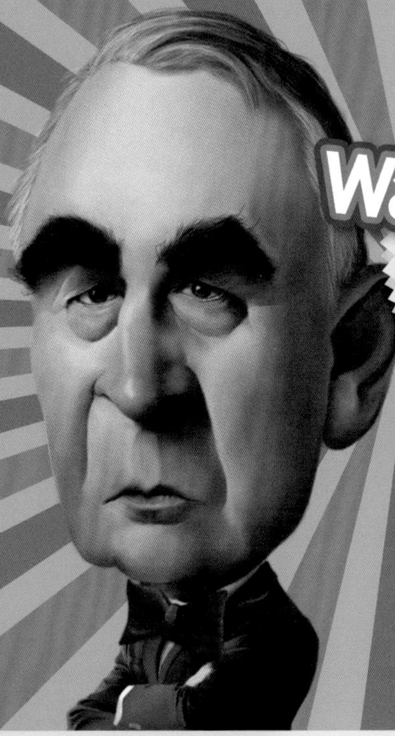

29TH PRESIDENT
Warren Gamaliel Harding
OF THE U.S.A.

★ **TERM** 1921 to 1923
★ **PARTY** Republican
★ **NICKNAME** The Happy Hooligan
★ **CLAIM TO FAME**
The Teapot Dome Scandal
★ **BORN** Caledonia, Ohio
★ **FIRST LADY** Florence Harding
(married 1891 to 1923)

"America's present need is not heroics, but healing; not nostrums, but normalcy."

Warren G. Harding

BIG-FOOT HAD NOTHING ON HARDING—THIS PREZ WORE A SIZE 14 SHOE!

Harding won the Oval Office by promising to end all that reform talk that Wilson liked. Harding wasn't looking to be "great," just loved. Unfortunately for him, he had little vision for the direction of the country, and he surrounded himself with some of the wrong people.

HANGIN' WITH THE WRONG CROWD

Some say the role of president was more of an honor than a job to Harding, and he generally let folks around him do what they wanted. When Congress wanted to strictly limit immigration, lower taxes for the rich, and bring back the high tariff, he signed on the line. In his time in office, he appointed some notable people

WHY HE'S WEIRD Harding loved poker. Maybe he was overconfident since he played so much; Harding once bet a set of White House china in a hand. He lost.

105

like former president Taft as Chief Justice of the United States and Herbert Hoover as secretary of commerce. But he also had some other buddies—the "Ohio Gang"—whose endless bribes and moneymaking schemes ended up ruining his reputation, even though Harding himself wasn't directly involved in any of it.

ONE LAST RIDE

As talk of scandal began to emerge, Harding decided to tour parts of the U.S. and explain his political policies. As the details of the scandals were breaking, so was Harding. He couldn't sleep at night, and he couldn't catch his breath.

Harding thought all the cramps, tummy troubles, and fevers were from food poisoning. Turns out it was stress, a heart condition, and pneumonia, which turned his goodwill tour into a goodbye tour. After his death in office, the Teapot Dome (see Oval Awful, left) scandal broke, and his reputation took a nosedive.

SHADOW OF A DOUBT

After Harding's death, people thought his wife, Florence Harding, behaved a bit oddly. She refused to let authorities perform an autopsy to determine the cause of death, she had his body embalmed within an hour, and raced home to burn many of their private papers. Experts later determined Harding died from natural causes, but that didn't stop some folks from suspecting foul play.

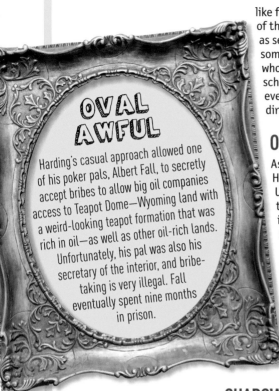

OVAL AWFUL

Harding's casual approach allowed one of his poker pals, Albert Fall, to secretly accept bribes to allow big oil companies access to Teapot Dome—Wyoming land with a weird-looking teapot formation that was rich in oil—as well as other oil-rich lands. Unfortunately, his pal was also his secretary of the interior, and bribe-taking is very illegal. Fall eventually spent nine months in prison.

FLORENCE HARDING: SIMPLY MISUNDERSTOOD?

30ᵗʰ PRESIDENT Calvin Coolidge OF THE U.S.A.

★ **TERM** 1923 to 1929
★ **PARTY** Republican
★ **NICKNAME** Silent Cal
★ **CLAIM TO FAME**
  Presiding over prosperity
★ **BORN** Plymouth Notch, Vermont
★ **FIRST LADY** Grace Coolidge
  (married 1905 to 1933)

"If the federal government were to go out of existence, the common run of people would not detect the difference."

CALVIN COOLIDGE LIKED TO START HIS **MORNING OFF RIGHT** BY **LUXURIATING** IN A **VASELINE HEAD MASSAGE.**

After the scandals that rocked Warren G. Harding's presidency, America wanted the strong, silent type. Enter Calvin Coolidge. On the inside, Calvin Coolidge wanted to hide if he heard a stranger's voice, but on the outside, he stayed cool, calm, and collected. He even won a second term with the slogan "Keep Cool With Coolidge." Not because he was movie-star cool, but because he always acted unruffled.

Coolidge was hands-off about everything. To this conservative, less government equaled a better government.

PRESIDENTIAL PETS Coolidge kept a pet raccoon named Rebecca and used to walk her on a leash!

WHY HE'S WEIRD!

COOLIDGE DIDN'T GET HIS NICKNAME, SILENT CAL, BY BEING CHATTY. AT A BORING WHITE HOUSE DINNER PARTY, A YOUNG WOMAN CONFESSED TO THE PRESIDENT THAT SHE'D MADE A BET THAT SHE COULD GET MORE THAN THREE WORDS OUT OF HIM. COOLIDGE RESPONDED SIMPLY: "YOU LOSE."

SMILE!
Despite his mute moniker, Silent Cal did not shy away from the public eye. Almost daily, the public had the opportunity to hear or see their leader during his weekly press conferences, monthly radio broadcasts, photo ops, and even a newsreel.

DOUBLY DEPRESSED

The 1920s roared under Coolidge with flappers, jazz music, and prosperity. It was even nicknamed "Coolidge Prosperity." Wages and jobs were up while the national debt was down. Consumer goods like radios and cars were flying off the production lines and into homes. Everyone was having fun, but then tragedy struck for Coolidge.

Coolidge's 16-year-old son died suddenly in 1924, and Coolidge admitted he was never the same. Some historians think he suffered from depression. Soon the state of the U.S. would match his mood.

COMMANDER IN NO RELIEF

Coolidge was so hands-off, he refused to pry into anyone's business—especially big business. This helped set the stage for the massive economic collapse known as the Great Depression.

Then one of the worst natural disasters in U.S. history to date happened—the flooding of the Mississippi River in 1927. Coolidge refused to send direct federal aid to the hundreds of thousands of desperate people. In his view, he'd just made a surplus for the government and he didn't want to use it all up!

Eventually, he and Congress agreed on some aid, and then Silent Cal issued a 10-word statement: "I do not choose to run for president in 1928."

Things were about to get really bad.

COOLIDGE STANDS IN THE BLACK HAT NEXT TO MEMBERS OF THE SIOUX TRIBE, 1925

31st PRESIDENT Herbert Hoover OF THE U.S.A.

★ **TERM** 1929 to 1933
★ **PARTY** Republican
★ **NICKNAME** The Great Engineer
★ **CLAIM TO FAME**
Presiding over the Great Depression
★ **BORN** West Branch, Iowa
★ **FIRST LADY** Lou Henry Hoover
(married 1899 to 1944)

> "We in America today are nearer to the final triumph over poverty than ever before in the history of any land."

Herbert Hoover

Herbert Hoover was never elected for anything until he became president. That's because he wasn't a politician. He was an engineer. A really rich one. To many voters, this self-made millionaire symbolized the American dream.

Orphaned before he was 10, Hoover bounced between family members before going to college to study geology. In the ultimate rags-to-riches story, he took jobs around the world consulting about mines, writing about mines, and buying mines.

With a campaign promise of "a chicken in every pot and two cars in every garage," Hoover won a gold mine: the presidency.

BURNING THE MIDNIGHT OIL

Hoover got right to work in Washington. In his first few months, he reformed civil service and helped save millions of acres of national parks and forests. He also tasked federal agents with outfoxing organized crime leader Al Capone, reformed the prison system, and set up commissions to survey police practices and the criminal justice system. Whew!

BUSTED

OVAL AWESOME Because he had made his own fortune, Hoover donated his presidential salary to charity.

BLACK (STOCK) MARKET

Hoover read the warning signs before the Great Depression hit. There were a number of causes for the massive economic crisis: drought, poor banking practices, and overproduction of goods, to name a few. Back in the 1920s, Hoover warned President Coolidge that the stock market (the system by which stocks—or shares—of a company are bought and sold) was out of control. It finally crashed (dramatically and suddenly lost value) on Black Tuesday, October 29th, 1929.

Many people lost their jobs and their homes. There was not enough work to go around and food prices skyrocketed. To add to the chaos, the Midwest was experiencing the worst drought in decades, turning farm soil into dust and causing constant "black blizzards" of dust. It was called the Dust Bowl, and while it hit in 1931, it would only get worse through the '30s, outlasting Hoover himself. The devastating dust storms hit Depression-era America right in the food-making region: the Midwest.

Thanks to more incentives from the government to farm differently, farmers had torn up the land to plant wheat instead of letting grass grow. When high winds and little rain came, there was nothing keeping the dust on the ground. It blew away, making ranching and farming impossible. Sixty percent of the population migrated out of the disaster zone.

A BAD ACT

Although more than a thousand economists begged him to stop, Hoover signed the Smoot-Hawley Tariff Act in 1930, which raised taxes on imported goods. He thought it would kick-start the economy by making people abroad want to buy American-made goods. Instead of

ALTHOUGH IT BEARS HIS NAME, THE **HOOVER DAM** OPENED WITHOUT **HOOVER** IN ATTENDANCE BECAUSE HE **WASN'T INVITED.**

FRUIT-FULL FRENZY

When Hoover first discovered the sweet taste of pears, he gorged on almost nothing else for two days straight. He made himself so sick that he didn't touch another pear for years!

110

helping the situation, Europe stopped trading with America because of the sky-high taxes and the economy went from bad to worse.

UNDER PRESSURE

Hoover decided to switch tactics. In 1932, he put together the Reconstruction Finance Commission (RFC) to lend money to banks, hoping they would lend it to businesses, and then hoping it would trickle down and stop the massive unemployment. It didn't.

Hoover's reluctance to assist Americans head-on stemmed from his belief that too much government help would make the country lose that do-it-yourself mentality that he felt made it great. He eventually succumbed to pressure and agreed to send the states money for direct relief. Even this aid came with strings attached, and Hoover believed it would only be temporary. He also did provide funds for some public works projects to create jobs for the unemployed.

Hoover was reluctant to see that this wasn't a tiny recession, and the wealthy weren't going to help the poor out of the goodness of their hearts. While he actually did more than any of his predecessors when faced with a financial panic, this big problem called for even bigger action.

NOT THE VACUUM CLEANER

The country sunk deeper and unemployment rose higher, eventually reaching 25 percent! Hoover, still claiming the end was around the corner, lost Americans'

PEOPLE SERVING SOUP AND BREAD IN LOS ANGELES DURING THE GREAT DEPRESSION

GAME ON!

TO KEEP HIS SVELTE FIGURE, HOOVER'S DOCTORS ORDERED HIM TO PLAY THEIR COMPLETELY MADE-UP GAME OF HOOVERBALL, NO SKILL REQUIRED. TO PLAY, HOOVER GOT TOGETHER A SIX-POUND (2.7-KG) MEDICINE BALL, A VOLLEYBALL COURT, AND A FEW FRIENDS. THE OBJECTIVE WAS TO HEAVE THE MEDICINE BALL UP AND OVER THE NET, THEN SCORE LIKE YOU WOULD A TENNIS MATCH. THE SPORT'S OFFICIAL ORGANIZATION THAT STILL EXISTS TODAY AGREES WITH *SPORTS ILLUSTRATED*, "THIS CANNOT BE ACCOMPLISHED GRACIOUSLY." OR GRACEFULLY.

faith that he could help. Not being a practiced politician hurt him, too, since he had trouble working with Congress. People cursed his name in breadlines (where people waited to receive free food) and in the cardboard-and-paper shantytowns that popped up all over the country. They sarcastically named the shantytowns Hoovervilles in his honor. The final straw came when World War I veterans marched to Washington, D.C., to ask for their veteran bonuses early. Many were disabled, had no homes to go back to, and nothing left in the hard times. Not only did Hoover tell them to leave, but he didn't control General Douglas MacArthur, who used deadly force on the protesters.

The great humanitarian went out the way he came in—in a landslide.

WHY HE'S WEIRD

While stationed in China, Hoover and his wife, Lou, learned enough Mandarin to be able to converse in secret. It came in quite handy during functions at the White House.

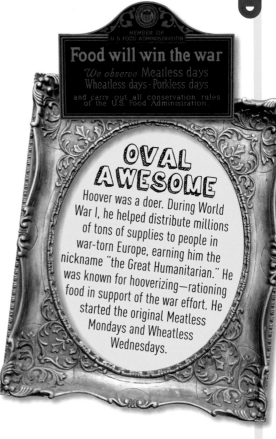

MEMBER OF
U.S. FOOD ADMINISTRATION

Food will win the war

We observe Meatless days
Wheatless days · Porkless days
and carry out all conservation rules
of the U.S. Food Administration.

OVAL AWESOME

Hoover was a doer. During World War I, he helped distribute millions of tons of supplies to people in war-torn Europe, earning him the nickname "the Great Humanitarian." He was known for hooverizing—rationing food in support of the war effort. He started the original Meatless Mondays and Wheatless Wednesdays.

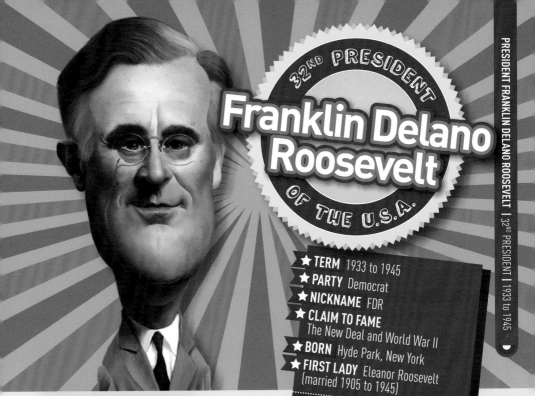

32ND PRESIDENT
Franklin Delano Roosevelt
OF THE U.S.A.

★ **TERM** 1933 to 1945
★ **PARTY** Democrat
★ **NICKNAME** FDR
★ **CLAIM TO FAME**
The New Deal and World War II
★ **BORN** Hyde Park, New York
★ **FIRST LADY** Eleanor Roosevelt
(married 1905 to 1945)

"The only thing we have to fear is fear itself."

Franklin D. Roosevelt

FDR IS THE ONLY **PRESIDENT** TO SERVE MORE THAN TWO TERMS— HE WAS **ELECTED FOUR TIMES!**

As an only child, historians say Franklin Roosevelt's mother was often overattentive. But the positive encouragement she gave him from a young age turned him into a confident man intent on changing the American presidency ... and he did just that.

DARK DAYS

Franklin Roosevelt took over the Oval Office during the dark days of the Great Depression. Many Americans had lost their life savings. As many as one-fourth of the population was out of work, and dozens of states had temporarily closed their banks or issued restrictions on how much money

PRESIDENTIAL PIZZAZZ When the king and queen of England visited America in 1939, President Roosevelt took them to a picnic and served them hot dogs!

people could take out. Almost half of the country's farmers were farmless. Nobody trusted the banks, and nobody knew how to fix the problem.

A NEW DEAL FOR OLD PROBLEMS

Roosevelt knew he had to do something fast. With the help of his Brains Trust—six academic friends he relied on for advice—FDR started throwing ideas at the problem.

Their first idea? A holiday! The day after his inauguration, Roosevelt declared a four-day bank holiday, meaning he shut down the entire U.S. banking system. This gave Roosevelt a chance to appear before Congress to push through the Emergency Banking Act. It promised to put more currency into circulation, so when people deposited their money, they didn't have to be afraid of it disappearing.

CHATTING IT UP

In his second week, Roosevelt chatted with the American people via the radio. He spoke directly to the citizens like old buddies hanging around his fireplace, but every detail down to his words and the speed of his delivery were carefully prepared.

Roosevelt's "Fireside Chats" were a blockbuster hit. In his first chat, he explained what was happening and urged everyone to trust him and trust the banks. Amazingly, people listened. Even though they were clamoring only a few days earlier in a mad dash to get their money out of the banks, they redeposited more than half the money they'd hoarded before the bank holiday. The bank holiday had worked!

In contrast to the 600 letters Hoover had received each day, Roosevelt got thousands. The people trusted him. Congress trusted him. Trust was his best deal yet.

CAMERA SHY

FDR SPENT WHAT WOULD TURN OUT TO BE THE LAST DAY HE COULD WALK DOING ALL SORTS OF SPORTY THINGS, LIKE SAILING, SWIMMING, AND EVEN PUTTING OUT A FOREST FIRE. THE NEXT MORNING, HIS LEG MUSCLES HURT. HE THOUGHT IT WAS ALL THAT RUNNING AROUND, BUT IT WAS REALLY POLIO-MYELITIS—A VIRUS THAT CAUSES PARALYSIS. HE'D NEVER WALK UNAIDED AGAIN. BECAUSE OF THIS, FDR ASKED THE PRESS TO NEVER FILM HIM BEING CARRIED, AND THEY AGREED! IF A TOURIST SNAPPED A CANDID SHOT, SECRET SERVICE WOULD SWOOP IN TO CONFISCATE THE CAMERA.

FDR IN A RARE PHOTOGRAPH THAT SHOWS HIM IN A WHEELCHAIR, 1941

THE 100-DAY TEST

Presidents today often try to follow FDR's 100-day test. They try to get lots done in the first 100 days, before the honeymoon with Congress and voters is a distant memory. What can you do in 100 days? Learn to play the piano? Teach your goldfish to sit and stay? Give it a shot!

UNPRECEDENTED PRESIDENT

FOR BETTER OR FOR WORSE, FDR SAW THE NATION THROUGH THE MOST DEVAS-TATING WAR THE WORLD HAD SEEN. THE U.S. AND ITS ALLIES (BRITAIN, THE SOVIET UNION, FRANCE, CANADA, AUSTRALIA, TO NAME A FEW) WOULD EVENTUALLY BE VICTORIOUS AFTER SIX GRUELING YEARS. IN THE MEANTIME, ROOSEVELT RAN FOR AN UNPRECEDENTED THIRD TERM IN 1940 AND WON, BUT HE DIDN'T STOP THERE. HE RAN AGAIN FOR A FOURTH TERM AND WON. *AGAIN.* LESS THAN THREE MONTHS INTO IT, HE DIED OF A BRAIN HEMORRHAGE. JUST TWO YEARS LATER, CONGRESS PROPOSED THE 22ND AMENDMENT TO RESTRICT PRESIDENTIAL TERMS TO TWO.

ALPHA-BETTING

Thanks to the Depression, the government finally took responsibility for the welfare of its citizens. Through Roosevelt's New Deal, Congress passed bills through both houses like they were passing notes in class—without looking and very quickly. Dubbed "alphabet soup" because of the various acronyms, there were serious perks to all the new bills and associations. One of Roosevelt's favorites was the CCC (the Civilian Conservation Corps). More than 2,500 camps full of young men spent their days hacking down trees, planting new ones, building and improving parks, building roads, and helping farmers. The men got to learn new skills and earn a paycheck, infrastructure was improved, and each state received desperately needed conservation help.

To make the market more flexible, Roosevelt took America off the Gold Standard, which means U.S. money no longer had value directly linked to gold. He also passed a bunch of farming and public works acts to create jobs. In all, during his first 100 days, Roosevelt signed 15 major bills into law.

The passing of the 21st Amendment repealed the 18th Amendment, officially ending Prohibition. People celebrated in the streets.

IN A SLUMP

All that work didn't stop another slump in the economy in 1937. This one was caused by some of Roosevelt's policies, such as cutting government spending, and taking new taxes out of people's paychecks for his Social Security program. Established in 1935, the Social Security Act provided aid to the elderly, retired, and people who were sick or otherwise unable to work. Everyone called it the "Roosevelt

Recession," and some began to wonder why they'd voted him in for another term.

On top of that, Europe was in economic trouble, too. The whole world was facing difficult times, which meant they were more vulnerable to corrupt leadership. Adolf Hitler wanted the all-white "Aryan race" of Germany to expand to the east and take over vast amounts of territory. Over the next few years, he nearly succeeded. In the South Pacific, Japan was on an imperial mission to take over surrounding territories, and they were gaining ground. There was a new war brewing.

Many Americans did not want to get involved. Look what happened last time, they said—some 50,000 American boys died in combat during World War I— and Europe was already back at it again.

Then, in 1941, the Japanese attack on Pearl Harbor changed everything.

PANIC IN THE PACIFIC

In a presidency spanning the Great Depression and World War II, there's bound to be a lot of low points, and Pearl Harbor was definitely one of them, for FDR and for the nation. On December 7, 1941, Japan launched a sneak attack on the Navy base at Pearl Harbor in Hawaii, killing almost 2,500 Americans, damaging or sinking eight battleships, and destroying about 160 planes. The nation was in shock. President Roosevelt declared war on Japan. Days later, Germany declared war on the United States, and the U.S. promptly returned the declaration.

ALL FIRED UP

After Pearl Harbor, America was in the thick of war, sending troops to the Pacific to fight Japan and, in 1944, to Europe to fight Hitler. Suddenly, there were tons of jobs and the economy got a major boost. Wartime production was at an all-time high as the country banded together to work against a common enemy.

STATE OF DELUSION

THE ATTACK ON PEARL HARBOR WAS SO JARRING THAT FDR RESPONDED WITH A KNEE-JERK REACTION. AFTER THE ATTACK, THE FBI ROUNDED UP MORE THAN 110,000 JAPANESE AMERICANS, WHETHER THEY WERE AMERICAN CITIZENS OR NOT, AND FORCED THEM INTO DETENTION CAMPS. AT CAMPS LIKE MANZANAR, IN CALIFORNIA, LIFE WAS REGULATED INTO WORK SCHEDULES. THERE WAS NO PRIVACY AND LIVING CONDITIONS WERE MEAGER AT BEST. ALMOST 50 YEARS LATER, THE CIVIL LIBERTIES ACT OF 1988 OFFERED AN OFFICIAL APOLOGY AND SOME FINANCIAL RESTITUTION ($20,000) TO THE SURVIVORS OF THESE CAMPS.

THE BOMBING OF PEARL HARBOR, 1941

TOO CLOSE FOR DISCOMFORT

Like all close friendships, FDR and his British best friend, Prime Minister Winston Churchill, shared their ideas. When FDR developed a plan for after the war, he couldn't wait to tell Churchill. Roosevelt wanted nations of the world to come together to solve their problems—without resorting to tanks and guns. He called it the United Nations.

Supposedly, as the story goes, FDR was so excited that he wheeled right into the room where his friend was staying at the White House. Churchill was standing there pink and naked from a hot shower, but that didn't stop FDR from talking, nor Churchill from listening. Churchill declared he loved the idea! Then he got dressed.

UNITING NATIONS

FDR died only months before the end of WWII and the finalization of the United Nations. Unlike Wilson's failed League of Nations, the United Nations made a strong enough start under FDR to have the U.S. and 49 other countries join during a conference in San Francisco, California, in June 1945. Today, 193 countries still keep the peace in the UN.

Roosevelt may have died before any of these victories, but he left a giant mark on the presidency. Never again would the president be a regular guy. The office of president of the United States had become one of the most high-profile positions in the world.

OVAL AWESOME

President Roosevelt appointed the first woman to a Cabinet post. Frances Perkins became his secretary of labor. She took part in all sorts of public works acts as well as the Social Security Act. She also drafted the rules for the first minimum wage, overtime pay, and unemployment benefits.

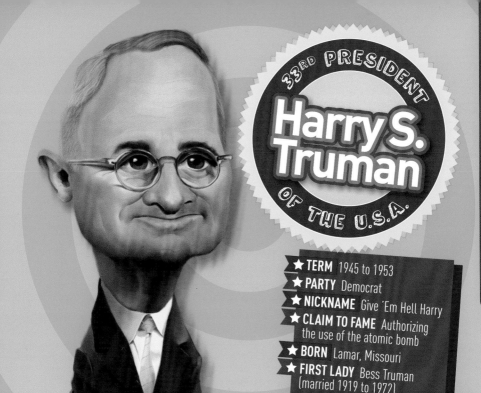

33RD PRESIDENT

Harry S. Truman

OF THE U.S.A.

- ★ **TERM** 1945 to 1953
- ★ **PARTY** Democrat
- ★ **NICKNAME** Give 'Em Hell Harry
- ★ **CLAIM TO FAME** Authorizing the use of the atomic bomb
- ★ **BORN** Lamar, Missouri
- ★ **FIRST LADY** Bess Truman (married 1919 to 1972)

"If you can't stand the heat, get out of the kitchen."

Harry Truman

Harry S. Truman was a sensitive soul who loved to read and play the piano, yet, this self-educated small-town boy would help define America's place in the world.

After only 82 days as FDR's vice president, Truman became president. It was the closing days of World War II and Truman had only talked to Roosevelt twice. Welcome to the White House, Mr. President!

TREADING WATER

FDR proved to be a tough act to follow, especially since Truman's only political experience involved sparring with politicians from Missouri and serving for 10 rather uneventful years in the U.S. Senate. Suddenly, in July 1945, this farm boy found himself in Berlin, Germany, at the Potsdam Conference, meeting with Soviet leader Joseph Stalin and British prime minister Winston Churchill, and later the new prime minister, Clement Attlee.

Hitler had died and World War II was coming to an end. Now the Allies only had to make world peace and

TRUMAN DIDN'T HAVE A **MIDDLE NAME—** THE **S** STANDS FOR HIS TWO GRAND-FATHERS, **SOLOMON** AND **SHIPP.**

NOT BOWLED OVER Truman's friends bought him a bowling alley and installed it in the West Wing as a birthday present in 1947, but he didn't much care for the sport.

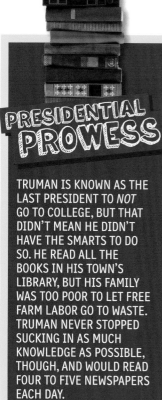

TRUMAN IS KNOWN AS THE LAST PRESIDENT TO *NOT* GO TO COLLEGE, BUT THAT DIDN'T MEAN HE DIDN'T HAVE THE SMARTS TO DO SO. HE READ ALL THE BOOKS IN HIS TOWN'S LIBRARY, BUT HIS FAMILY WAS TOO POOR TO LET FREE FARM LABOR GO TO WASTE. TRUMAN NEVER STOPPED SUCKING IN AS MUCH KNOWLEDGE AS POSSIBLE, THOUGH, AND WOULD READ FOUR TO FIVE NEWSPAPERS EACH DAY.

keep a third world war from happening, even though neither the U.S. nor Britain trusted Soviet leader Joseph Stalin. Among many postwar outcomes, Germany eventually was split into East and West Germany, and even the capital city Berlin was divided between the Allies!

BIG DECISIONS

At the end of the conference, the U.S., backed by Britain and China, drew up the Potsdam Declaration asking Japan to surrender or face total destruction. Truman received no response. Facing more war, the president made the drastic decision to utilize America's most powerful weapon: atomic bombs.

The two atomic bombs were dropped over the cities of Hiroshima on August 6 and Nagasaki on August 9, devastating the cities and killing hundreds of thousands of people. To this day, they are the only two nuclear weapons to have been used in a war. The Japanese emperor, Hirohito, surrendered almost immediately on August 14, 1945, shortly after the Soviet Union entered the war and the atomic bombs were dropped.

ISOLATION ON ICE

Truman decided America would no longer stand by and observe foreign affairs from afar during peacetime. The first thing the president did was pump money into war-torn Europe. The Truman Doctrine gave money to Greece and Turkey to counter Soviet Communism, while the Marshall Plan funded Western Europe. In theory, communism was the idea that wealth should be equally distributed to everyone, but in practice in the Soviet Union, communism meant that the Communist Party was in charge of every-thing and no democracy existed.

In 1948 Stalin tested how serious Truman was about protecting West Berlin by blockading the U.S., British, and French parts of Berlin. Truman responded by airlifting tons of food to the starving Berliners for over a year until Stalin lifted the blockade. Stalin and Truman had begun a very chilly game of politi-cal chess. It was called the Cold War.

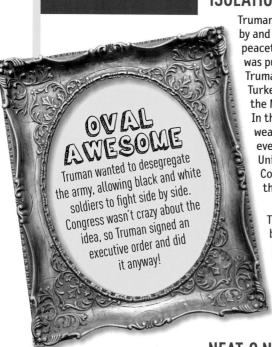

OVAL AWESOME

Truman wanted to desegregate the army, allowing black and white soldiers to fight side by side. Congress wasn't crazy about the idea, so Truman signed an executive order and did it anyway!

NEAT-O NATO

Truman considered NATO, or the North Atlantic Treaty Organization, one of his finer moments. Signed in

1949, it brought together Western European countries in a pact to defend each other if attacked.

STALLIN' STALIN

Another great war didn't sound good to anyone, especially when nuclear bombs were involved, but the U.S. and the Soviet Union were still on opposite ends of the spectrum when it came to political beliefs. In 1950, North Korea invaded South Korea. Stalin supported the communist North Korea and within two days, Truman, through the United Nations, sent troops to defend non-communist South Korea.

Since war was never officially declared, Truman didn't ask Congress's permission, but at the time containing communism was something most everyone was on board with.

THE CONSOLIDATOR!

America was now a global player, but it was also a tangled web of departments and duties. Truman realized the need to organize the jumbled mess. He consolidated departments and coordinated the sharing of information. In the process, he made the first peacetime spy agency (the CIA) and transformed the War Department into the Department of Defense.

A NEWER, FAIRER DEAL

On the home front, Truman wanted to take Roosevelt's New Deal even further. Immediately after the war he presented Congress with a 21-point plan

WHY HE'S WEIRD!

TRUMAN WAS, IN HIS OWN WORDS, "BLIND AS A BAT." BUT IN 1905 HE REALLY WANTED TO JOIN THE MILITARY, SO HE MEMORIZED THE EYE CHART IN ORDER TO PASS. IT WORKED, AND HE JOINED THE MISSOURI NATIONAL GUARD. HIS UNIT WAS CALLED UP DURING WORLD WAR I, AND AS CAPTAIN HE TURNED AN UNRULY BATTERY INTO A LEAN, MEAN FIGHTING MACHINE.

TRUMAN WAS THE UNDERDOG AND NEWSPAPERS KNEW IT. ONE PAPER EVEN PRINTED THE NEXT MORNING'S PAPER WITH THIS HEADLINE BEFORE RESULTS WERE TALLIED. WHOOPS!

of domestic improvements, many of which were also included in his 1949 "Fair Deal" speech. These proposals would increase minimum wage and unemployment benefits, and provide universal health care. His plan sounded a bit too close to communism for some. Congress wasn't impressed, and they failed to pass much of the legislation.

Next, Truman called for civil rights action. He became the first president to speak to the National Association for the Advancement of Colored People (NAACP). Truman had already issued an executive order forbidding discrimination in federal employment.

MISSING MISSOURI

Late in his presidency, Truman wasn't nearly as popular as his predecessor. He was tired of everyone questioning his decisions, including the Supreme Court and Congress. Meanwhile, the Korean War dragged on, and his ratings hit rock bottom.

After his second term, Truman decided enough was enough. He missed Missouri, so that's where this farmer boy went to retire.

PRESIDENTIAL PRECEDENTS

TRUMAN WAS THE FIRST PRESIDENT TO:
★ DESEGREGATE THE ARMED FORCES
★ ASK AMERICANS TO STOP EATING SO MUCH (IT WASN'T A HEALTH THING—IT WAS TO HELP HUNGRY EUROPEANS BY SENDING THEM FOOD)
★ BROADCAST AN INAUGURAL ADDRESS ON TELEVISION (WELL, TO THOSE WITH TELEVISIONS AT LEAST, WHICH WAS AROUND 1 IN 10 FAMILIES AT THE TIME)

PRESIDENTIAL PIZZAZZ

Before he was president, Truman opened a clothing store with a friend, but it failed miserably. The store folded after three years, but he still believed he had a great sense of style. He wore Hawaiian-print silk shirts on all his vacations and started a craze. He even appeared on the cover of *Life* magazine wearing one!

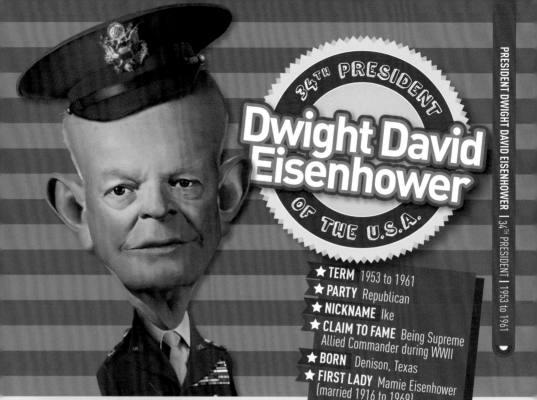

34TH PRESIDENT

Dwight David Eisenhower

OF THE U.S.A.

- ★ **TERM** 1953 to 1961
- ★ **PARTY** Republican
- ★ **NICKNAME** Ike
- ★ **CLAIM TO FAME** Being Supreme Allied Commander during WWII
- ★ **BORN** Denison, Texas
- ★ **FIRST LADY** Mamie Eisenhower (married 1916 to 1969)

"The supreme quality of leadership is integrity."

Dwight D. Eisenhower

EISENHOWER'S HIGH SCHOOL **CLASS VOTED HIS BROTHER** "MOST LIKELY TO BECOME PRESIDENT." EISENHOWER GOT "HISTORY PROFESSOR."

Although Dwight Eisenhower is known as the only president to serve in both World Wars, he never saw active combat. During World War I it was by chance: The war ended just a week before he was set to deploy. During World War II, it was by design: Eisenhower was a master military operations strategist. His work behind the scenes as Supreme Allied Commander meant he traveled the world but largely stayed off the battlefield and behind closed doors to plan the next move of the Allied forces (the U.S., Britain, and France, among others) against the Axis powers (including Germany, Italy, and Japan). He is largely known for masterminding the D-Day

PRESIDENTIAL PIZZAZZ War hero and fashion designer? Eisenhower designed the Ike Jacket, a "neater and smarter" field jacket that became standard issue for troops in 1944.

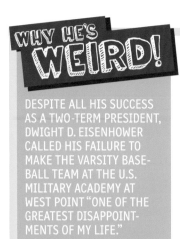

invasion of Normandy, and accepting the uncondi-tional surrender of Nazi Germany a year later.

Because of his operational strategy and skills, by the end of World War II, General Eisenhower was a very pop-ular man. Both Republicans and Democrats wanted him to be their presidential nominee. Even Harry Truman, who was president at the time, thought Eisenhower was the man for the job. He encouraged the military general to run on the Democratic ticket. But not one to take orders, Eisenhower aligned himself with the Republican Party, even though they hadn't been in the White House in 20 years. Ike liked their conservative spirit, and they liked Ike's track record of military success.

COLD SHOULDER

Like many people who experience war, Ike didn't like it. But the tension between America and the Soviet Union was growing. During World War II, the U.S. and the Soviet Union, which had opposing opinions of how the world should be run, set aside their differences to focus on defeating Germany. But now, with World War II in the rearview mirror, tensions between the two superpowers arose once again.

When Eisenhower became president, he wanted to keep America out of direct confrontation with the Soviet Union. Unfortunately, it was a little too late for that. In 1950, Soviet-backed North Korea had already invaded U.S.-backed South Korea, and President Truman had sent in troops under the banner of the UN. Still, Ike thought that communist nations threatened the American way of life. Ike sent more troops to Korea and then threatened "massive retaliatory power" in the form of nuclear warfare, and the confrontation in Korea finally ended. It also helped that in 1953, Joseph Stalin died and the

Soviet Union's new leadership was more amenable to working with the U.S. The so-called Cold War (as there was no physical warfare between the two countries) was not over, but tensions relaxed.

AMERICAN DREAMS

In 1956 Eisenhower was elected to a second term with the goal of keeping the peace abroad and focusing on nurturing a growing nation at home. He started the Interstate Highway System, oversaw Hawaiian and Alaskan statehood, and created the National Aeronautics and Space Administration (NASA).

The middle class was on the rise, but that didn't mean life in the 1950s was poodle-skirt perfect. Most of the comfy suburban homes that had popped up after the war had one other thing in common—they seemed to be full of only white people.

While Ike didn't speak out publicly in support of civil rights, he did sign into law the first civil rights bill since the post–Civil War Reconstruction period. The Civil Rights Act of 1957 outlawed discriminatory voting practices, but overall it was not considered a big step in the direction of equal rights and equal opportunities for African Americans.

COOL FOR SCHOOL

During this time, there was an active civil rights movement going on and up to this point, most schools in the American South had been segregated, meaning white kids went to one school and African-American kids to another. They were supposed to be "separate but equal," but most of the time that was not the case. On May 17, 1954, the Supreme Court passed the *Brown v. Board of Education of Topeka* ruling, which essentially said that separate but equal was not only not the reality in American life, but that it was also unconstitutional. Some people weren't happy with the ruling, and mobs threatened to physically hurt the African-American kids who tried to enter schools that attempted to desegregate. Many local leaders turned a blind eye to it, or even encouraged the behavior. But Ike got tough and serious. He sent the 101st Airborne to escort one group of kids in Arkansas to class— for the whole year.

SECRET OFFICE

IKE LET OFF STEAM BY GOLFING. HE WOULD LACE UP HIS GOLF SHOES IN THE OVAL OFFICE, TAKE A FEW PRACTICE SWINGS, AND THEN HIT HIS NEWLY INSTALLED PUTTING GREEN ON THE WHITE HOUSE LAWN. LATER, PRESIDENT RICHARD NIXON NEEDED TO REPLACE THE WOODEN FLOORS IN THE OVAL OFFICE BECAUSE OF ALL THE CLEAT MARKS IKE LEFT BEHIND!

THE RACE FOR SPACE

IN THE LATE 1950S, THE U.S. AND THE SOVIET UNION, STILL AT ODDS ON EARTH, SET THEIR SIGHTS HIGHER. THE SPACE RACE (THE COMPETITION BETWEEN THE TWO NATIONS TO DEVELOP SPACE TECHNOLOGY) WAS ON WHEN THE RUSSIANS LAUNCHED SPUTNIK IN 1957. IT WAS A LONE SATELLITE NO BIGGER THAN A BEACH BALL, BUT IT MADE QUITE A SPLASH.

THE POSSIBILITIES OF CONTROLLING THE AIR ABOVE EARTH WERE ENDLESS—AND IT LIT QUITE A FIRE UNDER AMERICAN SCIENTISTS! THEIR FIRST SATELLITE, EXPLORER, HIT THE SKIES ON JANUARY 31, 1958.

I SPY ...

With his hands full at home, the last thing Ike wanted was the Cold War to crank up the heat again. As a military mastermind he knew he needed to keep on top of world affairs, so he sent agents from the Central Intelligence Agency (CIA) on globe-trotting trips across the world to gather intelligence and report back home.

Unfortunately, in 1960 the U.S. was caught red-handed as an American spy plane was shot down over Russia. And the timing could not have been worse.

Eisenhower planned to meet with world leaders in Paris, including Soviet leader, Nikita Khrushchev, to talk about Cold War issues. Plans were going well until Khrushchev received word that an American U-2 spy plane had been captured over their airspace.

The U.S. tried to convince Khrushchev it was simply a meteorology (weather) plane, but the Soviets had all the evidence they needed, including the pilot, and pictures of the Soviet secrets the spy plane had in its possession.

Things looked bad. Eisenhower was caught in a lie heard 'round the world, but he refused to apologize and insisted the U.S. wouldn't have to snoop if Russia weren't so secretive.

The Cold War continued.

WHAT'S UP, DOC?

The spread of communism continued to be a problem late into Eisenhower's presidency. He was determined to contain it, and created the Eisenhower Doctrine, which promised to help any country that requested U.S. money or troops to fight communism.

Next, he endorsed CIA plans for an invasion of communist Cuba, which was a little too close to U.S. soil for comfort. But that wouldn't be his problem. He left that for the next president, John F. Kennedy.

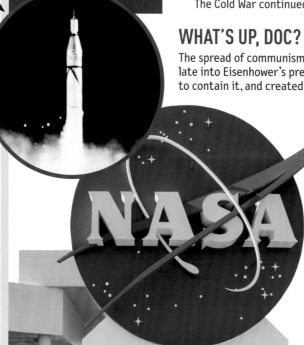

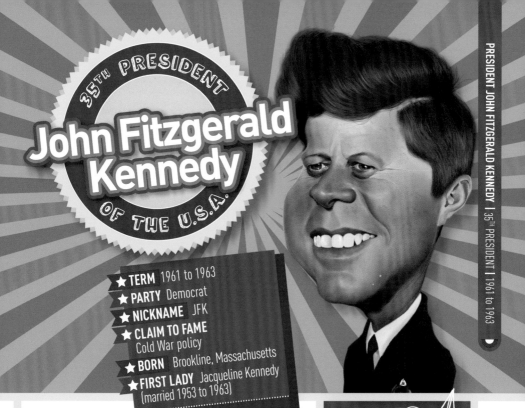

35TH PRESIDENT
John Fitzgerald Kennedy
OF THE U.S.A.

- ★ **TERM** 1961 to 1963
- ★ **PARTY** Democrat
- ★ **NICKNAME** JFK
- ★ **CLAIM TO FAME** Cold War policy
- ★ **BORN** Brookline, Massachusetts
- ★ **FIRST LADY** Jacqueline Kennedy (married 1953 to 1963)

"And so, my fellow Americans, ask not what your country can do for you; ask what you can do for your country."

John F. Kennedy oozed youth and good looks, which wasn't surprising since, at 43, he was the youngest president ever elected. Kennedy took to the spotlight like a moth to a flame, and lent an air of celebrity to the nation's highest office. Watching JFK, his glamorous wife, Jackie, and their adorable kids summering on Cape Cod, in Massachusetts, and rubbing elbows with the stars was captivating to the public. Everyone wanted to party with this prez!

Kennedy promised to give the American people not just tough talk, but tough action against Communism. But three months into his term, pigs flew. And they left a huge mess.

A PIGSTY

The Bay of Pigs Invasion in Cuba was a disaster. What had been started by Eisenhower landed in Kennedy's

DURING STRESSFUL **MEETINGS, KENNEDY** LIKED TO **DOODLE.** HIS SPECIALTY? **SHAPES** AND **SAILBOATS.**

PRESIDENTIAL PIZZAZZ JFK played the part of a celebrity well. He wore stylish sunglasses, drove a topless Thunderbird, and navigated ritzy sailboats with ease.

KENNEDY HAD ENOUGH MEDICAL PROBLEMS TO STAY OUT OF THE ARMY, BUT HE WAS DETERMINED TO SIGN UP. AFTER GRADUATING FROM HARVARD IN 1941, AND WITH THE HELP OF HIS INFLUENTIAL FATHER, HE JOINED THE U.S. NAVY. ONE NIGHT, WHILE HE WAS IN COMMAND OF A SMALL TORPEDO BOAT IN THE PACIFIC OCEAN, A JAPANESE SHIP ATTACKED HIS BOAT. KENNEDY LED THE 11 SURVIVORS ON A FIVE-HOUR SWIM TO AN ISLAND, DURING WHICH HE TOWED AN INJURED MAN BY CLENCHING THE MAN'S LIFE JACKET BETWEEN HIS TEETH! ONCE THEY REACHED THE ISLAND, KENNEDY SCRATCHED A MESSAGE ON A COCONUT AND GAVE IT TO A NATIVE TO SEND TO HIS BASE. THE U.S. NAVY PICKED UP THE SURVIVORS AFTER SEVEN DAYS. KENNEDY KEPT THE COCONUT ON HIS DESK IN THE OVAL OFFICE.

lap. A complex plan to overthrow the communist leader of Cuba, Fidel Castro, and his government ended as a full-blown catastrophe. If something could go wrong, it did. The CIA's plan was to equip Cubans in the United States with weapons and training and then support them as they landed in Cuba and tried to overthrow Castro. Squiggly lines on maps turned out to be swamps, time zones weren't coordinated between air and land forces, and the Cuban people, who were expected to help kick out Castro, didn't join forces with the U.S. Instead, American forces were captured, and the world knew the U.S. had tried and failed to start an uprising. In retrospect, Kennedy probably should've said no to the U.S. Navy code name for the mission: Bumpy Road. Kennedy accepted full blame, even though it wasn't his idea in the first place.

DICEY CRISES

JFK's problems in Cuba weren't over yet. The Bay of Pigs disaster led to Castro allowing Soviet leader, Nikita Khrushchev, to secretly transfer missiles to Cuba. The United States discovered that the Soviets were building these missile installations. With Cuba being a mere 90 miles (145 km) off the coast of the U.S., the not-so-secret Cuban-Soviet friendship had the U.S. reeling.

In retaliation, Kennedy blocked, or quarantined, Cuba's port with U.S. ships so no Soviet ships with missile equipment could make it to Cuba. It was sort of an old-fashioned standoff, only this time with nuclear weapons.

TO INFINITY AND THE MOON

The last great frontier in American eyes was space. Kennedy promised to have Americans on the moon by the end of the 1960s. NASA had a lot of work to do!

Fortunately, JFK and Khrushchev were able to work out their differences. Kennedy agreed to pull out old missiles in Turkey, and Khrushchev dismantled his in Cuba. For Kennedy, this was a huge political victory against the communist Soviet Union. That was a close one!

CLASH OF THE CONGRESSMEN

JFK had another problem, and this time, it wasn't Cuba. It was Congress. Many in Congress didn't like his ideas. That young whippersnapper wanted to combat poverty, use government money for better education, provide medical care for old people, and guarantee equal rights for all citizens.

Kennedy stuck to publicly approving of Brown v. Board of Education (see page 125), and he sent troops south to make sure kids got to class and that federal court decisions were enforced. He also called for a tough new civil rights law in mid-1963. But all his legislative failures were about to change. Unfortunately, this change didn't come about in the way anyone expected.

PRESIDENTIAL PRECEDENTS

KENNEDY WAS THE FIRST PRESIDENT TO:
★ BE BORN IN THE 20TH CENTURY
★ HAVE BOTH HIS MOM AND DAD AT HIS INAUGURATION
★ USE FLAMETHROWERS TO CLEAR AWAY SNOW DURING HIS INAUGURATION
★ INVITE A POET (ROBERT FROST) TO READ AT HIS INAUGURATION
★ BE CATHOLIC
★ ENGAGE IN TELEVISED DEBATES BEFORE HIS ELECTION
★ BE AWARDED A PULITZER PRIZE AND A PURPLE HEART (IN FACT, HE'S THE ONLY PRESIDENT TO WIN EITHER, LET ALONE BOTH)

WHY HE'S WEIRD!

JOHN F. KENNEDY WAS A JAMES BOND FANATIC. HE GUSHED UPON MEETING IAN FLEMING, BOND'S CREATOR, AND THEY EXCHANGED IDEAS ON HOW TO BRING DOWN CUBA'S DICTATOR, FIDEL CASTRO. IT'S SAID THAT ONE IDEA INCLUDED POISONING CASTRO TO MAKE HIS BEARD FALL OUT, SO HIS PEOPLE WOULDN'T RESPECT HIM ANYMORE. BEING A WRITER HIMSELF, APPARENTLY JFK PLOTTED HIS OWN SPY THRILLER, BUT HE NEVER RELEASED IT.

A NATION IN GRIEF

On a political trip to Texas, Kennedy rode through Dallas on November 22, 1963, in a convertible limo with the top down. The first lady sat next to him, waving to the crowds. As they drove through Dealey Plaza, he was shot and killed by Lee Harvey Oswald, a troubled man who believed in communism. A shocked America mourned deeply. It's estimated that a million people stood outside in Washington, D.C., to watch his funeral procession.

A LASTING LEGACY

Kennedy called on Americans to serve their country. He started the Peace Corps where volunteers traveled the world to help improve conditions abroad. He also put the federal government, with his June 1963 speech, firmly on the side of the growing civil rights movement.

America's golden boy left a lot of unfinished business behind, including a growing conflict around civil rights and another war that was brewing in Vietnam. It would be up to his vice president to push through his reforms.

John F. Kennedy said the 1960s would be a decade of change, and he was right. He just never got the chance to see how right he was.

OVAL AWESOME

The Cuban Missile Crisis had scared everyone. Kennedy turned down the Cold War thermometer by reminding the world that everyone wanted the same thing—to live. He secured a deal with Britain and the Soviet Union to end testing nuclear weapons in the atmosphere, reducing the chance of nuclear war.

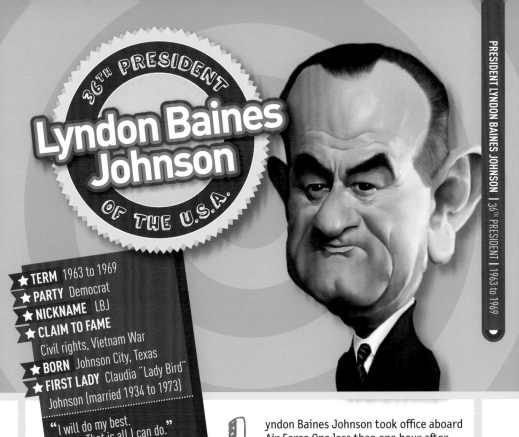

36TH PRESIDENT
Lyndon Baines Johnson
OF THE U.S.A.

* **TERM** 1963 to 1969
* **PARTY** Democrat
* **NICKNAME** LBJ
* **CLAIM TO FAME** Civil rights, Vietnam War
* **BORN** Johnson City, Texas
* **FIRST LADY** Claudia "Lady Bird" Johnson (married 1934 to 1973)

"I will do my best. That is all I can do."

Lyndon Baines Johnson took office aboard Air Force One less than one hour after Kennedy was killed. The vice president was all but too ready for the job. He seemed to go through life thinking he was the biggest and best around, second maybe only to his idol, Franklin D. Roosevelt.

Helping the poor and ending racial discrimination were high priorities, right next to steamrolling the opposition. But he didn't shy away from a challenge. Johnson wasn't afraid to confront issues head-on, which made his political "fall" later all the more shocking.

SHOCK AND AW(FUL)

Johnson had the gift of gab and could probably talk a dog into giving up a bone. This magic touch worked out especially well when it came to Congress. Johnson's strategy was one that he perfected when he was Senate leader in the 1950s. Called the Johnson Treatment, it's reported that LBJ used intimidation to bully legislators into getting his bills passed.

Apparently nothing was off the table during the Johnson Treatment, including middle-of-the-night phone calls, offensive jokes, not-so-subtle threats, and awkward conversations on the

HAIL TO THE CHIEF LBJ loved FDR so much, he turned his portrait to look at FDR's and captioned it "I Listen." He even occasionally wore pince-nez glasses to look more like his idol.

toilet. Historians say he wheeled and dealed like a car salesman. It got results. In his five years as president, Johnson pushed through 200 major laws.

FIRST-RATE GREAT

With chaotic energy, LBJ picked up on efforts Kennedy started, including the War on Poverty, ensuring health care for the elderly in the form of Medicare, and cleaning up America by signing almost 300 environment and conservation bills. Additional acts established more national parks, and gave our highways the royal beauty treatment. To give a billion dollars in aid to schools, he signed the Education Act of 1965 with his first teacher, Miss Katie, sitting next to him in the one-room schoolhouse he attended as a child. Then he created the National Endowment for the Arts to support theater, film, music, and art, and the National Endowment for Humanities to build libraries, museums, and colleges to house them in.

And that's just the highlights reel!

POOL PARTY!

Johnson called his vision the Great Society. It came from his time teaching underprivileged kids in Texas and from his desire to step out of Kennedy's shadow. LBJ loved being loved.

One overworked aide speculated that LBJ probably had "extra glands" that made him so energetic. For American history, it means he passed the first important civil rights bills since Reconstruction. The Civil Rights Act of 1964 ended segregation and

LBJ
GAVE EVERYONE IN THE FAMILY THE SAME
INITIALS. EVEN THE DOG,
LITTLE BEAGLE JOHNSON.

SECRET OFFICE

In addition to pushing legislators' buttons, LBJ installed two buttons on his Oval Office desk for drinks. They didn't dispense sugary soda themselves, but they did signal the valet to pour him either a soda or a coffee.

LBJ STANDING BETWEEN HIS WIFE AND JACKIE KENNEDY ON AIR FORCE ONE FOR A SWIFT SWEARING-IN CEREMONY, 1963

discrimination in public places like pools and libraries. The Voting Rights Act of 1965 finally provided strong measures to protect the voting rights of African-American citizens.

He partially had Kennedy to thank. Kennedy had pushed for a strong civil rights act in mid-1963. And, just like Garfield and Arthur 80 years before, the untimely death of the president helped spur a nation reluctant to change. Unfortunately, LBJ's victories were soon overshadowed by trouble abroad.

TROUBLE IN THE FAR EAST

The spread of communism was still a big concern, especially in developing countries. Truman, Eisenhower, Kennedy, and many Americans thought that if one country in Southeast Asia became communist, then they all would, so they'd been sending in "advisers" (aka soldiers) to help the non-communist South Vietnamese beat the communist North Vietnamese for years.

LBJ refused to be known as the president who lost Southeast Asia

PRESIDENTIAL PRECEDENTS

JOHNSON WAS THE FIRST PRESIDENT TO:
★ BE SWORN IN ON A PLANE
★ BE SWORN IN BY A WOMAN
★ APPOINT AN AFRICAN AMERICAN TO A CABINET POST (ROBERT C. WEAVER)

A WOMAN PROTESTS THE VIETNAM WAR IN NEW YORK CITY IN 1967.

STOP THE WAR IN VIETNAM NOW!

WHY HE'S WEIRD!

LBJ LIVED (AND DIED) BY THE EXPRESSION "THERE'S NO SUCH THING AS BAD PRESS." WHETHER HE BARED HIS SCARS IN PUBLIC, PULLED HIS DOGS UP BY THEIR EARS, OR BURPED AUDIBLY, HE WAS ALWAYS FEATURED IN THE DAY'S HEADLINES.

DAILY NEWS
BREAKING NEWS!!!

to communism. He kept ordering more bombs and troops to Vietnam, hoping South Vietnam could achieve victory. Even though he had once told America he was committed to keeping American boys out of foreign wars, by the end of his term, there were 535,000 troops on the ground, and the U.S. was fully embroiled in the Vietnam War.

Many Americans responded with fierce opposition. Protesters held demonstrations across the United States and some draft-eligible men fled the U.S. As a result of the protests, LBJ lost much of his influence over Congress.

RIDING OFF INTO THE SUNSET

Even though he could've technically run for another term, Johnson was tired. Morale was low. The Vietnam War was one of the most difficult and controversial wars yet, and it had sapped his strength. It didn't help that he was widely disliked by much of the public. Instead of wearing down congressmen, the charismatic Texas was worn down himself. LBJ retired to his ranch and died only a few hundred feet from where he was born, just a day before President Nixon announced that American involvement in the Vietnam War would soon end.

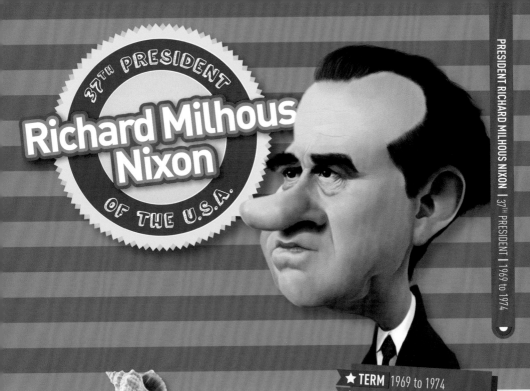

37ᵀᴴ PRESIDENT Richard Milhous Nixon OF THE U.S.A.

★ TERM	1969 to 1974
★ PARTY	Republican
★ NICKNAME	Tricky Dick
★ CLAIM TO FAME	Watergate
★ BORN	Yorba Linda, California
★ FIRST LADY	Pat Nixon (married 1940 to 1993)

"I am not a crook!"

NIXON ALWAYS WORE A **SUIT** AND **DRESS SHOES,** EVEN WHEN WALKING ALONG THE **BEACH.**

Richard Nixon had a lot of tricks up his sleeve. Historians say he played to win and wouldn't let much stand between him and victory. During his time in the Navy, he cleaned out his bunkmates playing poker until he'd squirreled away almost $7,000, which he used to fund his first political campaign. He won, of course.

Nixon used his intuition, smarts, and savvy to get all the way to the White House. He intended to make history remember his name, and boy did he ever.

WORSE FOR WEAR

Nixon's campaign included a plan to end the Vietnam War. As president, he ordered secret bombings of the country's neighbors, Cambodia and Laos, without asking

SECRET OFFICE As a law student, Nixon broke into the dean's office at Duke University to check his grades before they were posted.

MAKE ME UP

VICE PRESIDENT NIXON FIRST RAN FOR PRESIDENT IN 1960, BUT IT WAS HIS MISFORTUNE TO RUN AGAINST SENATOR JOHN F. KENNEDY AND DEBATE KENNEDY ON TELEVISION. JFK'S YOUTHFUL LOOKS AND POLISHED GRIN WON OVER THE CROWD. EVEN WORSE, NIXON DECLINED ANY MAKEUP. HE APPARENTLY LOOKED SO SICK ON THE SCREEN THAT HIS OWN MOTHER CALLED HIM LATER TO MAKE SURE HE WASN'T COMING DOWN WITH SOMETHING! PEOPLE WHO WATCHED THE DEBATE ON TV THOUGHT JFK HAD WON, WHILE THOSE WHO LISTENED ON THE RADIO THOUGHT NIXON HAD WON. IN THE END, KENNEDY PREVAILED, AND NIXON DIDN'T WIN THE PRESIDENCY UNTIL 1968.

Congress, continued the policy of training the South Vietnamese to become better fighters, and slowly began to pull out U.S. troops. He called the plan "Vietnamization." To make people at home happier, he also ended the draft. Boys weren't made to fight anymore just because they were over 18.

Still, the war dragged on. There were many antiwar rallies and marches. There were even some famous incidents where the National Guard and police fired on protesters at universities.

Finally, after decades of presidents believing that if one country fell to communism, the rest of the world would, Nixon decided enough was enough. He agreed to withdraw troops completely. The American experience in Vietnam was considered a failure, but at least it was over.

SEASONING WITH SALT

Nixon brought his poker face to the Cold War. He saw a wedge growing between communist friends China and Russia, and he decided to help the split along by squeezing himself in there.

NEW YORK

MOBILIZE TO STOP THE WAR IN VIETNAM

Saturday, April 15.

Assemble 11 a.m.
Central Park Sheep Meadow (66 St.)
March at noon to the United Nations.

CONNECT THE STATES

Nixon was the first president to visit all 50 states!

He traveled to Beijing, the capital of China, making him the first sitting U.S. president to visit the country, and met with leaders there, opening up the secretive country to trade and tourism with the U.S.

Nixon hoped to make the Soviets jealous, and it worked. Only three months later, Nixon got invited to Moscow, becoming the first U.S. president to visit the Russian capital. There, he signed the Strategic Arms Limitations Treaty (SALT), an agreement that limited the number of nuclear arms each country possessed. By showing that peace was possible with the Soviet Union, SALT set the table for later presidents.

HOME SWEET-SMELLING HOME

Nixon next set his sights on improving the home front. In order to stop America from becoming a dark land of polluted skies and garbage-filled lakes, he created the Environmental Protection Agency (EPA).

The Occupational Safety and Health Administration (OSHA) came next, and it helped protect workers on the job. Even wild animals also got some love. To ensure there would be cool creatures for generations to come, Nixon signed the Endangered Species Act.

SECRET SURVEILLANCE

Nixon's paranoia about his "enemies" began to increase when a military analyst decided to leak top secret documents about American military activities in Vietnam. The *New York Times* released what they called the Pentagon Papers to the American public. Starting with the Truman Administration, the 7,000-page document detailed all sorts of unsavory stuff that presidents really didn't want the public to know, like how they sometimes lied to get their way during war. People were shocked.

To Nixon, the release of the Pentagon Papers was scarier than the bogeyman. He wanted the Federal Bureau of Investigation (FBI) to teach the rat a lesson. They refused, so he hired people he called "Plumbers." Their job was to plug the leaks, and they resorted to some very

STATE OF DELUSION

BACK HOME, SOME MIGHT SAY THAT NIXON WAS ACTING WITH TOO MUCH POWER. HE SENT SPIES TO DIG UP DIRT ON HIS POLITICAL ENEMIES, ORDERED FINANCIAL REVIEWS OF COMPANIES THAT BAD-MOUTHED HIM, AND ILLEGALLY RECORDED PEOPLE'S CONVERSATIONS. HE EVEN ORDERED A SECRET SERVICE MAN TO TAP ALL OF HIS OWN BROTHER'S CALLS! HE WAS ALWAYS LOOKING FOR A SCANDAL TO SEAL THE DEAL ON HIS ENEMIES. IRONICALLY, THAT'S WHAT LED TO THE BIGGEST POLITICAL SCANDAL IN THE HISTORY OF POLITICAL SCANDALS: WATERGATE.

WATERGATE OFFICE COMPLEX, WASHINGTON, D.C.

ROAMING CHARGES

On June 20, 1969, Nixon made what's considered the "longest-distance" call ever. Nixon made a call all the way into space to congratulate Buzz Aldrin and Neil Armstrong for being the first men to walk on the moon!

illegal methods to accomplish their task. They broke into offices, stole files, and set bugs (listening devices) that secretly recorded conversations.

CREEPERS

Nixon wanted to build on what he'd done during his first term in office, so he ran for reelection in 1972. However, his Committee to Reelect the President (CREEP) included the Plumbers, and they treated the Constitution like a wad of crumpled paper.

One night in June 1972, they broke into the Watergate complex, where the Democrats housed their headquarters. They wanted to steal documents and bug more phones. But they were the world's worst wannabe robbers. The five crooks got caught, files in hand. This opened a hole the Plumbers couldn't plug: All their dirty tricks and secrets were eventually exposed to the world.

Nixon knew that having his own people caught in his opponent's headquarters in the middle of an election would look pretty bad, so he did his best to cover it all up.

FLOODGATES

The Watergate scandal became the world's biggest circus. As frantically as Nixon tried to cover up his cover-up of the break-in, reporters and the FBI were uncovering more details. Newspapers eventually revealed daily Nixon scandals—from lying on his taxes, to suitcases full of money paid to people who kept quiet, to using federal tax money to beautify the White House.

Watergate wasn't just about the failed break-in and the attempted cover-up: It opened the floodgates for all presidential misbehaviors. By mid-1973, years of presidential misdeeds sent the country into crisis.

THE ONLY WAY TO WIN

As early as 1940, presidents began secretly recording their Oval Office conversations. And in the spring of 1973, a Nixon aide revealed that President Nixon had been recording his conversations as well. Now, because of Watergate, everyone wanted to know what was on those tapes, and what else had been covered up.

Nixon claimed that because he was president he had the privilege to keep all his recorded conversations top secret, which started to look super suspicious. Even releasing a few tapes didn't help, because an 18.5-minute gap in one important conversation seemed a little long for a bathroom break.

WHY HE'S WEIRD!

THE FIRST BILLION TIMES NIXON ASKED HIS FUTURE WIFE ON A DATE, SHE TURNED HIM DOWN. TO NIXON, THAT JUST MEANT HE HAD TO TRY HARDER. HE RESORTED TO CHAUFFEURING HER AROUND ON DATES WITH OTHER GUYS UNTIL HE WORMED HIS WAY INTO HER HEART.

SECRET OFFICE

Nixon and his wife, Pat, loved bowling so much, they installed a brand-new one-lane alley under the driveway of the White House.

strike!

For most people, it proved he'd tampered with the tapes.

The House of Representatives started the impeachment process in 1974. Nixon decided to get out before that happened. He became the first U.S. president to resign. Some historians say that was the only way he had left to win. As for his legacy, Americans became more skeptical of their leadership. But history certainly remembers his name!

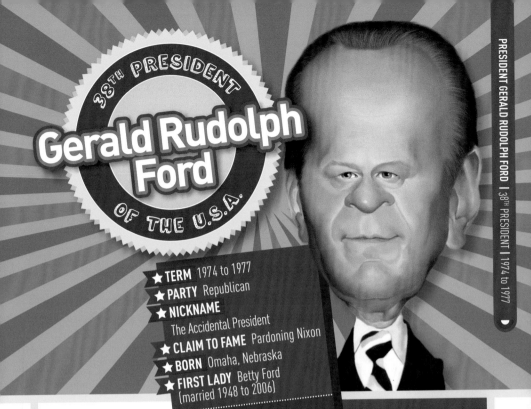

38TH PRESIDENT

Gerald Rudolph Ford

OF THE U.S.A.

★ **TERM** 1974 to 1977
★ **PARTY** Republican
★ **NICKNAME** The Accidental President
★ **CLAIM TO FAME** Pardoning Nixon
★ **BORN** Omaha, Nebraska
★ **FIRST LADY** Betty Ford (married 1948 to 2006)

"Our long national nightmare is over."

Gerald R. Ford

This all-American boy next door never expected to be president. As a congressman, Gerald Ford promised to run for one more term in Congress and then retire. Instead, he served 25 years. In 1973, President Nixon's vice president resigned, and Congress approved Ford as his replacement. Eight months later, Nixon resigned, making Ford the only president to not be elected to either office.

Ford's biggest problem wasn't his lack of legitimacy in the public's mind, though. For the most part, it was that people thought he was too *nice*.

FORGIVENESS FOLLIES

Ford wanted to doctor the nation back to good health after Nixon's Watergate scandal. The American public, however, was not exactly quick to forgive. When Ford pardoned the ex-president a month later— meaning Nixon would never go to trial or pay for any crimes he may have committed—people weren't

A YOUNG AND BLUE-EYED GERALD FORD ONCE MODELED FOR THE COVER OF A MAGAZINE!

Cosmopolitan

ALL TRIPPED UP Ford once got locked out of the White House while walking his dog!

WHY HE'S WEIRD!

GERALD FORD, A TERRIFIC FOOTBALL PLAYER AT THE UNIVERSITY OF MICHIGAN, WAS OFFERED A SPOT ON BOTH THE GREEN BAY PACKERS AND THE DETROIT LIONS NATIONAL FOOTBALL LEAGUE TEAMS. HE TURNED BOTH OF THEM DOWN AND WENT ON TO STUDY LAW INSTEAD.

pleased with the new president, and Congress was especially put off. Eight days later, Ford offered clemency, or leniency, to some men who'd refused to serve in the military (also called "draft-dodgers") during the controversial Vietnam War. This move angered some of the veterans who had fought. Ford's popularity never entirely recovered.

DEFYING DEATH

Ford's wide shoulders were for more than football pads and modeling gigs. During Ford's time in the Navy in World War II, they also helped him cling for dear life to the edge of his aircraft carrier during a typhoon. He narrowly avoided being tossed overboard. As president, he also survived two assassination attempts!

SQUEAKY CLEAN

Ford faced challenges that would have felled many presidents, and it didn't help that he hadn't actually been elected. But he did leave behind a lasting legacy for his honesty and integrity, despite his unpopular actions at the time. It wasn't enough to win a second term in the White House, but maybe it helped America believe in their government again after all.

FORD WITH HIS DOG, LIBERTY, BY HIS SIDE, 1974

OPERATION BABYLIFT

In a controversial move, President Ford had the U.S. government airlift some 2,000 displaced children out of war-torn South Vietnam at the end of the Vietnam War. These children were relocated and later adopted by families in the U.S. or its allied countries. However, many think not all of the children were actually orphans and that the relocation efforts separated some children from their families.

142

39TH PRESIDENT James Earl Carter, Jr. OF THE U.S.A.

★ **TERM** 1977 to 1981
★ **PARTY** Democrat
★ **NICKNAME** Jimmy
★ **CLAIM TO FAME** Energy, hostage, and confidence crises
★ **BORN** Plains, Georgia
★ **FIRST LADY** Rosalynn Carter (married 1946 to present)

"Our commitment to human rights must be absolute, our laws fair, our natural beauty preserved."

Jimmy Carter

As the former governor of Georgia, Jimmy Carter told America he wasn't a politician—he was a peanut farmer. But it was a good thing, because with a nation still reeling from scandal and war, this outsider was going to "clean up the mess in Washington." America liked the sound of that. Unfortunately, Washington, D.C., ended up being a tough peanut to crack, and his efforts often went unrewarded.

THE PEANUT GALLERY

After beating Gerald Ford in the election, Carter followed Ford's lead and pardoned all Vietnam War draft resisters. Now, draft resisters were no longer criminals for refusing to go to war. But just like Ford's decision, Carter's pardons angered some veterans.

Being an outsider hurt Carter with the Democratic Congress, as well. They didn't take him very seriously, and the two sides often had problems working together.

PRICEY PROBLEM

At home, the economy struggled. It had struggled throughout the 1970s. Unemployment was high, but so was inflation. Folks called this "stagflation."

WHY HE'S WEIRD Before he became president of the United States, Carter tried a laundry list of jobs, including cotton picker, naval officer, nuclear engineer, governor of Georgia, and peanut farmer!

GAS SHORTAGE! Sales Limited to 10 GALS. OF GAS PER CUSTOMER

That meant that prices for essentials like bread, eggs, and gas kept increasing. Carter struggled with fixing both issues and as time went on, people wondered if he should be fixing any of their problems.

EMPTY TANK

Carter's number one concern was energy. America was using tons of it to light their homes and drive their cars, and as a result, America was becoming dependent on oil from other countries.

To solve the problem, Carter had the forethought to look for alternative sources of energy and even created the Department of Energy to research wind and solar power. His bright ideas were largely scoffed at, much like the solar panels he put on the White House, which were taken down after he left.

DISASTROUS DIPLOMACY

Meanwhile, things were troubled on the international front. In November 1979, students in Iran took about 60 American hostages from the United States embassy in the capital city Tehran. The immediate cause was that President Carter allowed a disgraced Iranian political leader who had been ousted from their country to seek medical treatment in the U.S.

Carter tried the diplomatic route with peace talks, then the not-so-diplomatic route with military force. Unfortunately, both were disasters. In 1980, Carter authorized a secret military rescue, but a few choppers got stuck in a sandstorm, others had mechanical failures, and one collided with another aircraft, killing eight soldiers. Worse still, Iran found top secret info in the wreckage. And none of the 52 remaining hostages were rescued.

CARTER (COULD) SPEED-READ AT A RATE OF 2,000 WORDS A MINUTE.

NOT GOING FOR THE GOLD

The Soviet Union invaded Afghanistan in December 1979 to ensure the country stayed pro-Soviet. To Carter, this was a big problem. He responded by refusing to sell the Soviets any grain. But this hurt American farmers, who lost a big customer. Then Carter asked for a boycott of the 1980 Summer Games that were being held in Moscow, the Soviet capital. The U.S. Olympic Committee agreed with the president and Congress.

PEACE PRESIDENT

Amid the chaos, Jimmy Carter had a few successes with his foreign policies. He established official diplomatic ties with China, which allowed American manufacturers and buyers to purchase cheaper products and materials. And, in a somewhat controversial move, Carter signed a treaty to return control of the Panama Canal to Panama, beginning on December 31, 1999.

Carter also brought leaders from longtime rival countries Israel and Egypt to Camp David, the presidential country retreat. He wanted to help them hash out their issues—and it worked! The Camp David Accords established peace between Israel and Egypt for the first time in history.

CANDID CAMERA

DURING A VACATION, CARTER WENT FISHING. IT WAS GOING WELL—UNTIL THE "ATTACK" OF A WILD SWAMP RABBIT! THE LITTLE GUY KEPT SWIMMING CLOSER. CARTER CLAIMED IT WAS HISSING AT HIM AND SPLASHED IT AWAY WITH HIS PADDLE. A WHITE HOUSE PHOTOGRAPHER CAUGHT IT ALL ON CAMERA, AND CARTER NEVER LIVED DOWN THE STORY OF THE SCARY SWAMP RABBIT.

PRESIDENT JIMMY CARTER BETWEEN EGYPTIAN PRESIDENT ANWAR SADAT AND ISRAELI PRIME MINISTER MENACHEM BEGIN AT THE WHITE HOUSE, 1978

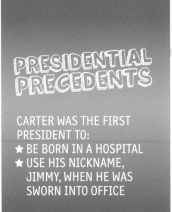

PRESIDENTIAL PRECEDENTS

CARTER WAS THE FIRST PRESIDENT TO:
★ BE BORN IN A HOSPITAL
★ USE HIS NICKNAME, JIMMY, WHEN HE WAS SWORN INTO OFFICE

PRESIDENTIAL SOUND BITE

In the summer of 1979, a gloomy but determined Carter told Americans that they had a "crisis in confidence" in themselves and in their government and that they spent too much on themselves. Everyone needed to "obey the speed limit and to set your thermostats to save fuel." Maybe walk to the store once in a while!

DOOM AND GLOOM

Jimmy Carter got a lot of bad press as president, but today, historians have warmed up to him. They say he faced issues with steady courage. In his day, though, he came across as a bit of a downer. Once an eternally optimistic movie star named Ronald Reagan decided to run against him, it was over for Carter's presidency.

The Iran hostages situation was the last thing to kick Carter while he was down. After Carter footed the legwork behind the scenes, Iran agreed to release the hostages after 444 days—but they waited until after Reagan's swearing in on inauguration day, making it look like Reagan had secured their safety.

DAILY NEWS

JOY OF FREEDOM

Hostages fly to Germany crying 'God Bless America'

WELCOME BACK TO FREEDOM

OPEN

THE HOSTAGES COME HOME!

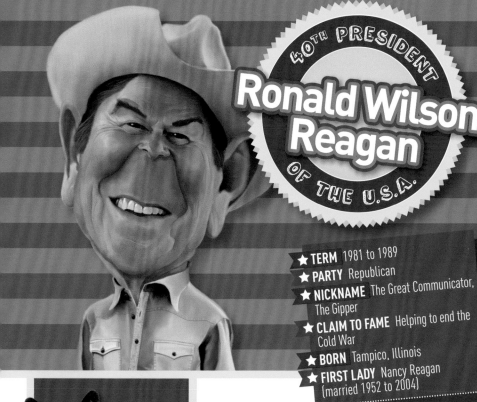

40TH PRESIDENT
Ronald Wilson Reagan
OF THE U.S.A.

★ **TERM** 1981 to 1989

★ **PARTY** Republican

★ **NICKNAME** The Great Communicator, The Gipper

★ **CLAIM TO FAME** Helping to end the Cold War

★ **BORN** Tampico, Illinois

★ **FIRST LADY** Nancy Reagan (married 1952 to 2004)

"Mr. Gorbachev, tear down this wall!"

Ronald Reagan

Like the dashing leading men he played in the movies, Ronald Reagan was warm and inviting. He believed in the American dream and made Americans believe in it, too. He was called the Great Communicator for his persuasion skills, and it often seemed that nothing could bring down his popularity. He left office a beloved president.

REAGAN WAS LEGALLY BLIND —HE HAD 20/200 VISION!

LESS IS BEST

Reagan didn't always win, but when he did, it was by a landslide. In 1980 many Americans were tired of Jimmy Carter, and they bought what Reagan was selling: a bright future. He won 44 of 50 states in 1980, and 49 of 50 states in 1984!

OVAL AWESOME Ronald Reagan appointed the first woman to the Supreme Court! Sandra Day O'Connor served from 1981 until her retirement in 2006.

Win one for the Gipper
Ronald Reagan

Even though a huge recession was stalling the economy, Reagan said he had a plan. He campaigned on a platform of less government, less taxes, less national debt, and a stronger stance against the Soviet Union. To Reagan, heavy taxation and government regulations were hindering American freedom.

REAGANOMICS

For the first time since the Great Depression, Reagan changed the way the government worked to help the economy with his "Reaganomics" program. His whole less-is-more approach included cutting taxes and slashing government programs. He was optimistic that the end of the rocky economic times was near.

But there was a catch: Many argued that the tax cuts helped the wealthy and big corporations much more than the average person. Reagan thought money would trickle down and eventually help everyone, but the gap between the wealthy and the poor grew wider during his presidency.

Reaganomics began to backfire. For the first time ever, the national debt went over $1 trillion. Then it went over $2 trillion. It almost reached $3 trillion before the end of Reagan's presidency. However, the country started to come out of the "Reagan Recession" in late 1982, and the overall economy and stock market were experiencing growth. This helped Reagan win reelection in 1984.

STAR POWER

REAGAN HONED HIS GREAT COMMUNICATOR SKILLS AS AN ACTOR IN HOLLYWOOD, APPEARING IN 53 MOVIES OVER HIS CAREER. IN HIS MOST FAMOUS ROLE, HE PLAYED A DYING FOOTBALL PLAYER NAMED GEORGE GIPP. ON HIS DEATHBED, GIPP ASKS THE TEAM TO "WIN ONE FOR THE GIPPER." REAGAN GOT A LOT OF MILEAGE OUT OF THIS LINE DURING HIS CAMPAIGNS, AND THE NICKNAME STUCK.

INTERNATIONAL SQUADRON
RONALD REAGAN
OLYMPE BRADNA · WILLIAM LUNDIGAN
JOAN PERRY · REGINALD DENNY
LEWIS SEILER
WARNER BROS.
THEY'LL CLIMB TO ANY CEILING IN A FLIGHT! THEY'LL REACH FOR ANY DANGER IN A FIGHT!!

PRESIDENTIAL SOUND BITE

Reagan wanted to tear down the emotional walls separating the Soviet Union and America in part by tearing down the physical walls that had fenced off the communist section of Berlin, Germany, since 1961. In a 1988 speech at the Berlin Wall, he asked the Soviet leader, Mikhail Gorbachev, to help end the Cold War by saying, "Mr. Gorbachev, tear down this wall!" The Berlin Wall "fell" in 1989 and people were finally free to travel back and forth.

MAY THE FORCE BE WITH YOU

It's no secret that this actor turned president liked the movies. Reagan called the Soviet Union an "evil empire" and wanted an expensive missile-defense system to protect America. People nicknamed his idea "Star Wars" because his system included lasers that would destroy enemy missiles in the air, just like in the movie, and the president pumped a lot of money into it.

To Reagan, the only way to end the Cold War was to be the stronger nation. In his first term, Reagan made some people nervous that his "peace through strength" policy would heat up the Cold War to nuclear levels. Luckily, the Soviet leader, Mikhail Gorbachev, who took over in 1985 was reform-minded. In other words, he wanted to tone down the Cold War and open up Soviet society.

Gorbachev and Reagan became friends and both agreed to no more nuclear buildup and signed the Intermediate-Range Nuclear Forces (INF) Treaty in 1987. It was the first time in history that the two political giants had agreed to reduce their nuclear weapons, instead of just stopping production of more weapons.

As for Reagan's Star Wars program, it ended up not being very practical or sustainable. Future presidents scaled the program back and redefined it.

PRESIDENT RONALD REAGAN CHIPS AWAY AT THE BERLIN WALL.

WHY HE'S WEIRD!

TO MAKE MONEY AS A YOUNG MAN, RONALD REAGAN BECAME A LIFEGUARD. HE WAS PAID $15 A WEEK PLUS ALL THE CONCESSION STAND FOOD HE COULD STOMACH. OVER SEVEN YEARS, HE SAVED 77 PEOPLE! BUT THAT'S NOT ALL. ONE TIME, A MAN OFFERED REAGAN $10 TO DIVE IN AND FIND HIS FALSE TEETH!

UNTOUCHABLE

There was still a great deal of public enthusiasm for the star president, despite some scandals. When word broke in 1986 that the U.S. was secretly selling weapons to Iran to free hostages in Lebanon, and then giving the cash to rebel fighters in Nicaragua to fight the communist government there, Reagan had to answer some tough questions. Instead, he answered, "I don't recall," and his underlings took all the blame. Many Americans didn't believe that Reagan could be so "in the dark" about things happening in his administration, and the Iran-Contra scandal damaged his popularity. However, he still left office with the highest approval rating of any modern president.

ONCE UPON A TIME

Today, many people still go gaga for the Gipper. They say he created almost 20 million new jobs, cut unemployment nearly in half, and jump-started the end of the Cold War. The longest recorded peacetime prosperity also occurred under his leadership. But critics point out the huge debt he left behind ($2.9 trillion) and the fact that the new jobs were mostly low-paying retail service jobs.

Reagan retired to his California home with his wife, Nancy, where he later revealed he suffered from Alzheimer's disease, which causes debilitating memory loss. Ever the optimist, he used his popularity to raise money for a cure, but eventually succumbed to the illness in 2004.

OVAL AWFUL

Only 69 days after Reagan's inauguration, a man named John Hinckley, Jr., shot the president. Reagan was rushed to the hospital, but he managed to stay conscious. Before surgery, he told the doctors, "I hope you're all Republicans!" His funny one-liners, even in an emergency, made much of the public adore him.

41ˢᵗ PRESIDENT
George Herbert Walker Bush
OF THE U.S.A.

★ **TERM** 1989 to 1993
★ **PARTY** Republican
★ **NICKNAME** Poppy
★ **CLAIM TO FAME** The Gulf War
★ **BORN** Milton, Massachusetts
★ **FIRST LADY** Barbara Bush (married 1945 to present)

"I want a kinder and gentler nation."

Gy Bush

George Herbert Walker Bush had a storied career, long before he even entered the Oval Office. During World War II, he was one of the youngest naval pilots ever, earning his wings shortly before his 19th birthday. During a mission over the Pacific, the Avenger bomber that Bush flew was hit by Japanese antiaircraft fire, but he still finished his mission. His plane crashed into the ocean and the two other crew members died. Bush, wounded, parachuted into the ocean. While bobbing on a life raft, a Japanese boat came to capture him. But American planes held off the Japanese and Bush held off the jellyfish long enough for him to be rescued by a submarine.

Bush's father, Prescott, was a wealthy businessman and politician. So, after serving in the military, George went into the oil business, became a millionaire, and then jumped into politics. Between being an ambassador to the United Nations and China, a congressman, director of the CIA, and vice president to Ronald Reagan, Bush knew a bit about politics and foreign affairs. But all that experience didn't matter when the economy struck again.

sweet!

PRESIDENTIAL PIZZAZZ Bush's dog, Millie, had her own room at the White House. It was previously Nancy Reagan's beauty parlor!

AS CAPTAIN OF YALE'S BASEBALL TEAM, BUSH MET BABE RUTH!

CHINESE PROTESTERS SUPPORTING THE PRO-DEMOCRACY MOVEMENT IN BEIJING, 1989

THOROUGHLY THOUGHTFUL

In 1989, there was political unrest in China. Pro-democracy protesters were speaking out against the communist government, and the government responded with deadly force. To stop what China thought was dangerous talk of democracy, the government used tanks and guns against protesters in Tiananmen Square in 1989, killing hundreds of demonstrators. While Bush hated the violence and publicly criticized the Chinese government, he also secretly sent diplomats to keep an open relationship. The talks allowed him to preserve trade relations.

NO TEARS

Foreign victories for Bush came in 1991 when the Soviet Union officially collapsed without a war or an invasion. Communist leaders in nearby European countries had already stepped down in the previous two years, as pro-democratic movements had swept communism from power. In October 1990, Germany was once again united as one country for the first time since World War II.

Although many in his party wanted him to, Bush didn't gloat over the collapse—he said he wasn't "an emotional kind of guy." Really, he didn't want to be a poor winner, which helped his reputation as a diplomat.

LET'S GET TOGETHER

Next, Bush focused on uniting countries in the Middle East for a common cause. When the dictator of Iraq, Saddam Hussein, ordered the invasion of the neighboring country, Kuwait, Bush spoke out against this "naked aggression"—meaning he thought the real reason Iraq invaded Kuwait was to take control of valuable oil fields.

President Bush wasted no time. He made four dozen cold calls to world leaders in five days. He wrangled money and men to lead a coalition of nations into war against Iraq. He even got the Soviet Union to side with the U.S. against Saddam Hussein. Some believe this joint statement issued by the U.S. and Soviet Union was the real end of the Cold War.

Once troops hit the ground, Operation Desert Storm only lasted 100 hours, and it ushered in the high-tech era of war. It featured live broadcasts from the front lines, a massive air strike, and footage of cruise missiles and "smart" bombs destroying their targets.

In the end, 148 Americans were killed. Saddam left Kuwait, and Bush was praised. However, some people criticized him for not chasing Saddam back to Iraq and throwing him out of power completely, while others protested the war altogether. They asked why the president would fight to defend a country that wasn't a democracy, saying the real reason was for Kuwait's oil.

WHY HE'S WEIRD!

AS PRESIDENT, GEORGE BUSH LOVED TO SPORT SOME FLASHY SOCKS, INCLUDING AMERICAN FLAG SOCKS, SUPERMAN SOCKS, AND EVEN A PAIR WITH HIS OWN FACE ON THEM!

FRENCH ARMED FORCES HELICOPTERS DURING THE GULF WAR, 1990

BROCCOLI BAN

BEING THE PRESIDENT MEANS NEVER HAVING TO EAT BROCCOLI AGAIN. ACCORDING TO BUSH, AT LEAST. HE REPORTEDLY BANNED THE GREEN STUFF FROM AIR FORCE ONE. "I'M PRESIDENT, AND I'M NOT GOING TO EAT ANY MORE BROCCOLI!" HE DECLARED.

HOME FRONT

As if there weren't enough problems in the world, the home front had plenty to keep Bush busy, too. Domestic affairs weren't necessarily his strong suit. Instead of working with the Democratic Congress, he tried to work around them. He used his veto powers regularly, and he fought anything that seemed like too much government interference.

Of course, he did sign some important bills. The Americans with Disabilities Act made it illegal to discriminate against anyone with a disability in public places or in workplaces, while the Clean Air and Water Act worked to lower smog, toxic chemicals, and acid rain in the environment.

A TAXING DECISION

Reagan left a huge debt behind, but in his campaign, Bush promised the people, "Read my lips: no new taxes!" That put him in a pickle. One way to pay off the debt was to raise taxes, so he did, but people weren't happy about the promise-breaking.

His opponent in the next election, Bill Clinton, used it against him.

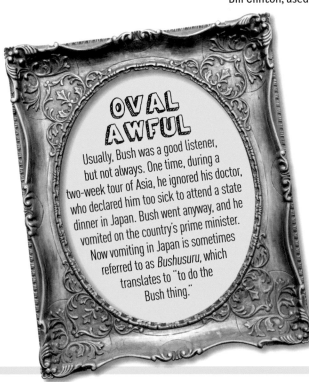

OVAL AWFUL

Usually, Bush was a good listener, but not always. One time, during a two-week tour of Asia, he ignored his doctor, who declared him too sick to attend a state dinner in Japan. Bush went anyway, and he vomited on the country's prime minister. Now vomiting in Japan is sometimes referred to as *Bushusuru*, which translates to "to do the Bush thing."

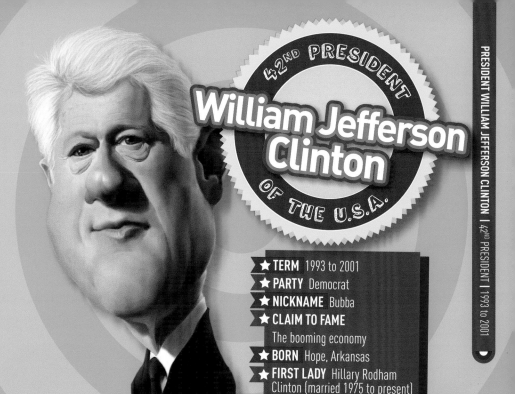

42ND PRESIDENT
William Jefferson Clinton
OF THE U.S.A.

- ★ **TERM** 1993 to 2001
- ★ **PARTY** Democrat
- ★ **NICKNAME** Bubba
- ★ **CLAIM TO FAME**
  The booming economy
- ★ **BORN** Hope, Arkansas
- ★ **FIRST LADY** Hillary Rodham
  Clinton (married 1975 to present)

"There is nothing wrong with
America that cannot be cured
by what is right with America."

William Clinton

Historians tout Bill Clinton as a smart president, but his legacy was somewhat overshadowed by in-office scandals. He is only the second U.S. president to ever be impeached (after Andrew Johnson). It had been so long since Johnson's impeachment trials in 1868 that members of Congress supposedly had to go to the National Archives to dust off handwritten documents by the nation's Founding Fathers just to figure out how to do it!

Despite all those problems, Clinton's presidency survived the trial. The Senate found him not guilty and he managed to leave office with one of the highest approval ratings in modern history.

HIGH SCHOOL HOPES

Growing up in Hope and Hot Springs, Arkansas, young Bill Clinton always had high

AS A KID,
CLINTON'S FAVORITE CATCH-PHRASE
WAS
"HOT DOG!"

PRESIDENTIAL PIZZAZZ  Bill Clinton jazzed up the presidential race by playing his saxophone on popular television programs. He even won awards for his tunes.

aspirations. After meeting with JFK at the White House in 1963, a high-school-age Clinton hoped to one day make it all the way to the Oval Office. By billing himself as a moderate "New Democrat," he promised changes the middle class wanted. Changes like taxes for the rich and stricter crime laws.

A BAD BILL OF HEALTH

During his first two years as president, Clinton wanted universal health care, which would've made medical treatment more affordable for everyone. Clinton put the first lady, Hillary, in charge of spearheading this plan.

People were not used to having the wife of the president take control of serious issues. Advisers shied away from their roles, not knowing if it was okay to give constructive criticism to the first lady. People felt the resulting proposal was overly complicated and confusing. Some commented that Hillary Clinton had not been elected to office, nor had she been approved by the Senate, like Cabinet officers. After 20 months of debates, the Clintons' big dream collapsed.

DON'T ASK

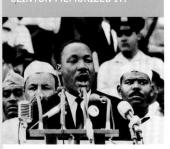

Besides his focus on health care, Clinton also wanted to end the ban on gay people in the military. Clinton was a supporter of gay rights, and he felt the military's views were outdated. Congress made him compromise, with the infamous Don't Ask, Don't Tell policy. Gay people could be in the military, but they couldn't say they were gay, and no one could ask them if they were. The compromise didn't make many people in either camp very happy.

One thing was certainly going right in Clinton's first term: the health of the economy.

NATIONAL TREASURE-Y

Clinton campaigned with the promise to fix the economy, balance the budget, and give the middle class a break on taxes. He even kept a sign over his campaign headquarters that read, "It's the economy, stupid."

Clinton didn't end up cutting taxes for the middle class as he had planned. Instead, he confronted a bigger-than-anticipated deficit, and was forced to raise some taxes in 1993. He wanted to cut the deficit, and eventually the debt. The national debt is different than the deficit. The debt is all the money

A PROTEST OUTSIDE CONGRESS BY THOSE AGAINST THE DON'T ASK, DON'T TELL POLICY

the country owes. The deficit refers to one year only. If the country spends more than it makes, there's a deficit for the year. The deficit is then added to the debt.

For the first time since Lyndon Johnson, the government had no deficit and even made money from 1998 to 2001. This is called having a surplus. Besides having a surplus, Clinton also paid off part of the national debt.

To do this, Clinton raised taxes on the rich and cut some government programs. After a recession during the Bush presidency, the economy bounced back strongly, with low unemployment and low inflation.

SHUTDOWN SHOWDOWN

Despite all this, Republicans in Congress fought against Clinton. In 1995, a Republican-controlled Congress forced a shutdown of the government to make Clinton do what they wanted and sign a budget bill. In the standoff, Clinton didn't blink (or sign), and Congress finally backed down.

People blamed Congress for the stalemate and reelected Clinton to a second term.

AGREEMENT = ACHIEVEMENT

Republicans and Clinton may have butted heads, but they actually agreed on a few things, whether they wanted to admit it or not. Even though it started out

PRESIDENTIAL PRECEDENTS

CLINTON WAS THE FIRST PRESIDENT TO:
★ BE BORN DURING THE BABY BOOM (THE YEARS FOLLOWING WORLD WAR II, WHEN THE BIRTH RATE SHOT UP!)
★ EARN A RHODES SCHOLARSHIP (THE *ONLY* PRESIDENT, TOO!)
★ BROADCAST HIS INAUGURATION LIVE ON THE INTERNET

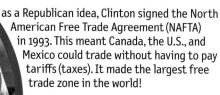

as a Republican idea, Clinton signed the North American Free Trade Agreement (NAFTA) in 1993. This meant Canada, the U.S., and Mexico could trade without having to pay tariffs (taxes). It made the largest free trade zone in the world!

Clinton also reformed welfare in 1996. Now, anyone who received help from the federal government in the form of welfare had to work within two years of receiving benefits, and they could only receive federal benefits for a maximum of five years.

TROUBLE ABROAD

While Clinton's ambassadors helped stop the warring between Northern Ireland and the U.K., they failed to bring peace to the Palestinian people and Israel, who had long been at odds in the Middle East. The violence there got worse.

Violence also worsened in Africa. President Bush had first sent troops into the eastern African nation of Somalia in December 1992 to aid starving people and help bring order. President Clinton continued with this policy, but he and his team weren't prepared for the intense civil war there. When the brutal fighting included the deaths of American soldiers, Clinton pulled out the rest in March 1994. A month later in Rwanda, Africa, there was a terrible genocide in which one ethnic group or national group killed another ethnic or national group.

WHY HE'S WEIRD

Bill Clinton loved McDonald's. He'd jog there, eat, and then jog home.

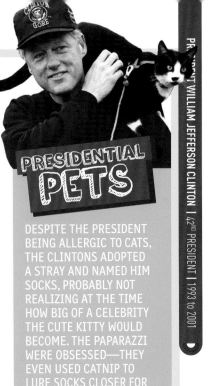

Up to 800,000 people died in 100 days, but Clinton, coming off the recent failure in Somalia, didn't do anything to stop it. The United States and many other countries were criticized for not stepping in to help.

Two years later, Clinton decided it was not a time to be timid with foreign policy. There was a civil war going on between different ethnic groups within the country of what used to be Yugoslavia. One group, the Serbs, was trying to rid the region of the two other groups, Muslims and Croats. Clinton pressured the world to send a strong message to the Serbs, to stop forcing the other groups out of the region. Over the next few years, NATO, the North Atlantic Treaty Organization made up of countries in North America and Europe, agreed to send weapons and aircraft to stop them.

PRESIDENTIAL PETS

DESPITE THE PRESIDENT BEING ALLERGIC TO CATS, THE CLINTONS ADOPTED A STRAY AND NAMED HIM SOCKS, PROBABLY NOT REALIZING AT THE TIME HOW BIG OF A CELEBRITY THE CUTE KITTY WOULD BECOME. THE PAPARAZZI WERE OBSESSED—THEY EVEN USED CATNIP TO LURE SOCKS CLOSER FOR A BETTER SHOT!

TROUBLE IN THE WHITE HOUSE

Meanwhile, Clinton was in the middle of a scandal at home. He had an affair with a young woman who worked in the White House, and the public found out about the relationship. Even worse, many believed he lied under oath about the affair, and lying under oath is illegal. The Republican Congress got ready to impeach a president for just the second time in American history. But some members, and many Americans, argued that Clinton's misconduct did not rise to the level of "high crimes and misdemeanors."

The House of Representatives voted to impeach him. The Senate acquitted, or forgave, him.

IT'S THE ECONOMY!

During Clinton's time in office, some 22 million jobs were created. He pushed anticrime laws through Congress to put more police officers on the street and passed the Brady Bill that requires buyers to get a background check before purchasing a gun.

He proved that strong domestic policy can trump scandal, and even impeachment couldn't keep him down. He left office after two terms with most of the public on his side.

George Walker Bush

OF THE U.S.A.

★ **TERM** 2001 to 2009
★ **PARTY** Republican
★ **NICKNAME** Dubya (W.)
★ **CLAIM TO FAME** War on Terror
★ **BORN** New Haven, Connecticut
★ **FIRST LADY** Laura Bush
(married 1977 to present)

"States like these, and their terrorist allies, constitute an axis of evil, arming to threaten the peace of the world."

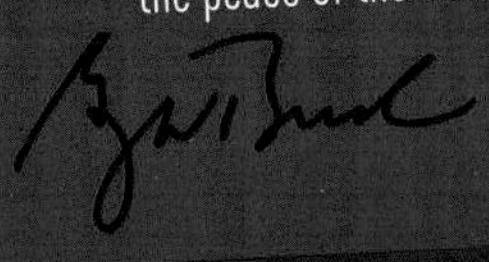

VACATION NATION Bush was known as the "vacation president," taking 533 days off for ▶▶▶

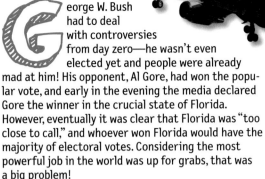

George W. Bush had to deal with controversies from day zero—he wasn't even elected yet and people were already mad at him! His opponent, Al Gore, had won the popular vote, and early in the evening the media declared Gore the winner in the crucial state of Florida. However, eventually it was clear that Florida was "too close to call," and whoever won Florida would have the majority of electoral votes. Considering the most powerful job in the world was up for grabs, that was a big problem!

BOGUS BALLOTS

After the first tally, Bush led by a small margin in the Sunshine State, but then some people stepped forward and said they'd voted for the wrong person by accident because the ballots were hard to read. The Democrat Al Gore was listed second, but voters seemingly had to punch out the third hole to vote for him. There were problems with ballot counting in other counties in Florida, and reports of voter intimidation. The entire presidency rested on recounting some of the ballots.

For 36 days, the nation (and the world) waited to see who would become the next president. Bush and Gore each pled their case to the media and to the courts. Eventually, the Supreme Court got involved. They decided by a 5–4 vote that Bush was not receiving equal protection and due process under the Constitution, and they ordered the recounts to halt. Bush had won Florida—and, therefore, he had won the presidency. Winning by default didn't exactly give Bush the united start he wanted.

BUSH LOVED TO RUN SO MUCH HE KEPT A TREADMILL ON AIR FORCE ONE AND RAN DURING FLIGHTS!

relaxation. While it sounds nice, presidents are still expected to work while on vacation.

9/11

Less than eight months after his inauguration, Bush faced perhaps one of the largest trials of any president in recent memory. On September 11, 2001, 19 men hijacked four planes from three different airports on the East Coast. They crashed two into the World Trade Center in New York City. They flew into the Pentagon building in Arlington, Virginia. Passengers on the fourth plane fought back, crashing it into a field in Pennsylvania. Almost 3,000 people perished that day, and many of the rescue workers from that time still face the effects from hazardous conditions resulting from the wreckage.

The attack began the largest criminal investigation in American history. It took only 72 hours for the FBI to identify the hijackers. They were all part of an extremist organization called al Qaeda, and their leader, Osama bin Laden, vowed to keep striking at America.

Bush's response to this terrorism would change not only the presidency, but the world.

OVAL AWESOME

Bush's Cabinet included people from diverse backgrounds. He appointed the first African-American woman to be secretary of state and the first Asian-American woman to a Cabinet position! While running for the presidency, Bush had said, "I'm smart enough to know what I don't know." So he hoped to fill his Cabinet with people who did.

TRANSFORMER

Bush sent troops to Afghanistan to find and capture terrorists. He declared a War on Terror and asked Congress to pass the USA Patriot Act only six weeks after the attacks. Airports put intense security checks in place, and Bush created a whole new office, the Department of Homeland Security, to prevent more attacks.

The controversial Patriot Act gave the government broad power to investigate suspected terrorists and stop their activities. The government could even read the library records of anyone they deemed suspicious, which many felt was an invasion of privacy. In just a few weeks, Bush made the presidential role more powerful than ever before.

SLAM-DUNKED

Bush then sent troops to Iraq to oust Saddam Hussein, the brutal dictator there, and because there were reports that Iraq had weapons of mass destruction (WMDs)—chemical, biological, or nuclear weapons that could do widespread damage. Bush and his team thought the case was a "slam dunk." But when the U.S. went in, they found no WMDs, and it turned out that the intelligence reports had been wrong. Hussein was captured and put on trial in Iraq and executed for his crimes. But the long war and inability to find the WMDs left Bush empty-handed and looking caught red-handed. People questioned the motives behind the Iraqi invasion, and so far no one has proved that Saddam had a direct link to the 9/11 attacks.

PASSION FOR COMPASSION

Bush campaigned as a "compassionate conservative," which meant he wanted to help people in conservative ways—like less government—but he was open to social changes. He initiated the biggest expansion of Medicare, which provides health insurance for people over 65, since Lyndon Baines Johnson created the program in 1965. Bush also tried to reform Social Security, but could never get the support he needed.

NO CHILD LEFT BEHIND

As the governor of Texas, Bush pushed for education reform, and he got it. Now he wanted to do it for the rest of the country. In a rare moment of cooperation, Bush got the Democrats and Republicans to work together to create the first education reform bill since LBJ's presidency. The No Child Left Behind Act created standards every school had to follow in order to make sure all kids received quality education. (Yes, including those dreaded standardized tests!)

DISASTROUS RESPONSE

In 2005, one of the most destructive hurricanes to ever hit the U.S. struck the Gulf Coast. By the time it was over, 80 percent of New Orleans, Louisiana, was underwater, displacing people and destroying homes.

The president had put the Federal Emergency Management Agency (FEMA) on the highest alert before the storm hit, but they were still accused of being underprepared and too slow to act. By some estimates, almost 2,000 people died, and tens of thousands more were without water, food, shelter, or even a bathroom. Thousands took refuge in the Superdome, a football stadium. For almost a week, they waited—without many basic human necessities—until they could be evacuated.

For many, FEMA, and by extension, the president, had failed at the moment of crisis. Bush had been on vacation and didn't realize at first how terrible the effects of Hurricane Katrina had been. He later admitted he wasn't quick enough in his response.

But the troubles didn't end there. The biggest recession since the Great Depression was around the corner.

CRASHING FURTHER

BUSH IN NEW ORLEANS, LOUISIANA, AFTER HURRICANE KATRINA

The Great Recession started in 2007 and many people were to blame for it. The housing market had been booming for years, but it was slowing down in 2006. Banks were practically giving away homes by loaning to people who couldn't pay the money back, and nobody was reining them in because lots of people were making money! When people couldn't pay back their loans, the banks were close to collapsing all together. That wasn't all. Corruption on Wall Street, where stocks are traded, was running rampant, and in the late summer and fall of 2008 the

STATE OF CONFUSION

WHILE CONDUCTING A PRESS CONFERENCE IN IRAQ, A REPORTER TOOK OFF HIS SHOES AND LOBBED THEM AT PRESIDENT BUSH. IN IRAQ, SHOE-THROWING IS THE GREATEST SIGN OF DISRESPECT. BUSH MANAGED TO DUCK BOTH, HOWEVER, AND LATER JOKED, "IF YOU WANT THE FACTS, IT'S A SIZE 10 SHOE THAT HE THREW."

stock market began declining, at times violently, putting many Americans' life savings at risk.

To top it all off, Bush pushed through tax cuts but didn't reduce government spending. Those tax cuts lowered taxes on almost all Americans, but many argued they mostly benefited the wealthy and widened income inequality. And all this happened while the U.S. was spending heavily on defense because it was engaged in two extremely expensive wars overseas.

By the end of the year, it seemed like the economy was on the brink of collapse. To keep the big banks and other industry alive, Bush came up with the Troubled Asset Relief Plan (TARP). It gave $700 billion to keep things up and running. But the work of fixing the economy would be mostly left to his successor, since not even Bush's own party voted for any of his programs anymore. Even the next Republican candidate didn't want Bush's endorsement. Bush became somewhat of a political outcast—even though some economic experts say if he hadn't acted with the "bailout," the recession could have been much worse.

A BAD BREAK

Some of Bush's most important legacies were overshadowed by the Iraq War and Katrina. One of his successes was the work he did with AIDS, a deadly, contagious disease. He helped get medications to people with the disease, saving millions of people with the program, which is still at work in Africa.

Despite some victories, and being voted in for a second term, Bush went from having the highest approval rating of any president when entering office to nearly the lowest when leaving.

44TH PRESIDENT

Barack Hussein Obama

OF THE U.S.A

★ **TERM** 2009 to 2017

★ **PARTY** Democrat

★ **NICKNAME** Barry

★ **CLAIM TO FAME** Affordable Care Act

★ **BORN** Honolulu, Hawaii

★ **FIRST LADY** Michelle Obama
(married 1992 to present)

"Change will not come if we
wait for some other person or
some other time. We are the
ones we've been waiting for.
We are the change that we seek."

THE COOL PREZ Instead of weekly fireside chats over radio waves like FDR had, Obama uploaded weekly videos to the Internet on Saturday mornings. Now the White ▶▶▶

OBAMA HAS READ ALL SEVEN HARRY POTTER BOOKS TO HIS DAUGHTERS.

O bama was the face of hope for America. Literally, "hope" was his campaign slogan. He had plenty to be hopeful about, including the great American spirit of change. It was this spirit that helped him make history as the first African American to run for president on a major political party's ticket. And it was also this spirit that made him the first African American to win. He had hope for the future and that wasn't going to change!

SCARY SITUATION (ROOM)

Two days after his election, Obama got the presidential goods: an intelligence briefing of all the top secret stuff a president needs to know. According to reports, he said, "I'm inheriting a world that could blow up any minute in half a dozen different ways." Now he was in charge of two wars and a massive recession—and that's not to mention all of his own policy changes he wanted to enact for America!

GETTING LIMBER

The presidency may be a marathon, but Obama started out sprinting. Americans were pretty worried about the direction of the country, and historians note that Obama wasn't just commander in chief; he had to be therapist in chief, too. Reassuring the nervous nation was right up there with fixing the economy, which is exactly what he focused on first. Many Americans were also nervous that Bush had hurt relationships with other countries during his War on Terror, and it was up to Obama to put them back on track.

WHY HE'S WEIRD!

EVEN AS OBAMA WAS RUNNING FOR PRESIDENT, HE REFUSED TO OBSESSIVELY WATCH THE NEWS. INSTEAD, HE PREFERRED WATCHING SPORTS. OBAMA ESPECIALLY LOVED BASKETBALL, AND HE MADE IT A HABIT TO PLAY EVERY ELECTION MORNING.

House even has its own YouTube channel!

LINK TO LINCOLN

OBADA CHOSE TO USE THE SAME BIBLE THAT LINCOLN USED AT HIS INAUGURATION 148 YEARS EARLIER. NO OTHER PRESIDENT HAD USED IT SINCE LINCOLN HIMSELF.

SPIDEY SENSES SAVE THE DAY

Obama loves to collect comic books, especially Spider-Man ones, so the creators put his inauguration in their January 2009 issue!

TARP TACTIC

Before he even took office, Obama approved of Bush's TARP plan, which lent $700 billion to banks and car companies to keep them from going under. After a fight with Republicans in Congress, Obama also initiated his own stimulus package: $800 billion for state governments, public works projects, and tax incentives for individuals and businesses. This was supposed to create jobs and save existing ones so unemployment wouldn't rise higher.

Next, he banned forms of harsh treatment for prisoners of war (which helped reassure the world that America wouldn't use torture), passed a bill to try to give equal pay to women, and laid the groundwork for reforming health care. And he wasn't through yet!

DOCTORING HEALTH CARE

Obama's biggest goal was to get health care that regular folks could afford. Almost 50 million Americans didn't have health insurance, and for some families, going to the doctor for anything— from a yearly check-up to severe illness—was nearly impossible. They simply didn't have the money to pay for health insurance or cover the costs of treatment. He wanted to regulate insurance companies so they couldn't charge people an arm and a leg for coverage. The new plan would also make it illegal for insurance companies to drop coverage of sick people.

But this sort of major change can create enemies—political ones. The Republicans in Congress wanted less government in people's lives, and they pointed out the high costs of the new program.

The two sides were about to be locked in an epic struggle.

COUNTERSTRIKE

Obama went to work. He addressed the nation about his plan and pounded the congressional pavement up and down Capitol Hill, meeting face-to-face with members of Congress.

In March 2010, Obama signed his big dream into reality. He called it the Affordable Care Act, but his critics dubbed it "Obamacare," and they wasted no time in striking back. Within seven minutes, 13 states sued the federal government for forcing every individual to buy insurance. The states claimed the new law was unconstitutional, meaning President Obama couldn't make them accept it.

BREWING POLITICS

Some Republicans who didn't like Obama formed a new conservative political group called the Tea Party that wanted the government to have less power. They named themselves after the original Boston Tea Party in 1773, which protested British taxes. The modern Tea Party was against the Obama Administration's decision to give financial aid to bankrupt homeowners, among other government programs.

In 2010, the Republicans took control of the House of Representatives. Obama's ability to get bills through Congress was about to get a lot harder.

RAISE THE ROOF

By 2011, with the debt having already greatly increased over the previous eight years, and due to the stimulus plan and Obamacare, the national debt was at an all-time high. Usually, Congress just agrees to raise the debt ceiling, which is the amount of debt a government can have. Many conservative Republicans didn't think that was a great policy, though, and they refused to agree to raise the number. In a nail-biting battle of power, negotiations went down to the very last minute before a compromise was reached. This was a big relief because not raising the debt ceiling could have led to big economic problems.

Then, Congress ruled that Obamacare was constitutional. It looked like Obama was finally catching a break!

SHUT DOWN

In 2013, Congress was at it again. That October, when Republicans and Democrats couldn't find a compromise over government spending, the government shut down for 16 days. Federal institutions, such as National Parks and post offices, closed, and employees weren't paid until politicians compromised.

TOP SECRET MISSION

Obama also had tough foreign affairs to deal with, like the two wars in the Middle East. By 2012, Obama pulled out all but 150 noncombat troops from Iraq. The decision was controversial, but it helped that in May 2011 Navy SEALs (a special operations force) acted on Obama's command to strike at a compound in Pakistan where Osama bin Laden, mastermind of the 9/11 attacks, was thought to be hiding. There were lots of risks involved, but when bin Laden was killed in the attack, America was grateful to have a conclusion.

DEPARTURE AND DISARRAY

Obama sent many troops into battle. He gave the military greater authority in Afghanistan to root out the rest of the Taliban (which brutally ruled Afghanistan until being overthrown by the U.S. in late 2001). He also was part of a NATO effort to protect civilians and aid democratic forces against Libyan dictator Muammar Gaddafi in Libya during the Libyan Civil War. But many argue that his office underestimated the

PRESIDENTIAL PRECEDENTS

OBAMA WAS THE FIRST PRESIDENT TO:
★ BE OF AFRICAN-AMERICAN HERITAGE
★ HAVE A TWITTER ACCOUNT
★ APPEAR ON A LATE-NIGHT COMEDY SHOW AS THE SITTING PRESIDENT
★ ADDRESS U.K. PARLIAMENT IN WESTMINSTER HALL
★ ENDORSE SAME-SEX MARRIAGE

vast reach and abilities of other terrorist groups in Syria, Iraq, and other areas. In the wake of U.S. troop withdrawal from Iraq, civil unrest and protests in other Middle Eastern nations were on the rise.

The Islamic State of Iraq and Syria (ISIS), another terrorist group, began to take control of sections of the Middle East, leaving a path of destruction in their wake. By the time Obama and other world leaders realized how powerful ISIS had become it was too late: ISIS was a powerful entity, and one the world is still fighting.

OPENING DOORS

For the first time since Eisenhower shut down diplomatic contact with Cuba in 1961, the United States opened an embassy there in 2015. As an encore, Obama took a trip to the country, becoming the first sitting president to visit Cuba since Coolidge in 1928.

Then he went to Hiroshima, Japan, making him the first sitting president to visit a city devastated by one of the two nuclear bombs dropped during World War II. His visit began a long-overdue healing process between the two countries over the U.S.'s use of nuclear weapons in WWII.

OVAL AWESOME
Obama received the Nobel Peace Prize in 2009 for his "efforts to strengthen international diplomacy."

POLITICS AS USUAL

Obama campaigned by promising to try to bridge the divide between the political parties that was threatening to split the country, but the divisions grew over his two terms. Both Democrats and Republicans dug in—deep.

This self-proclaimed "skinny kid with a funny name" changed history, and not just by being the first African-American president. His domestic plans and foreign policies shook up America, even if plenty of people are still divided about them. But that's just part of the job description!

45TH PRESIDENT
Donald John Trump
OF THE U.S.A.

★ **TERM** 2017 to present
★ **PARTY** Republican
★ **NICKNAME** The Donald
★ **CLAIM TO FAME** Being a business mogul
★ **BORN** Queens, New York
★ **FIRST LADY** Melania Trump (married 2005 to present)

"Our country, our people, our laws have to be our top priority again."

UNPREDICTABLE PREZ After the election, Trump refused daily security briefings, tweeted at celebrities and politicians, took unprecedented calls from world leaders, ▶▶▶

DONALD TRUMP IS THE ONLY PRESIDENT TO **NOT** HAVE ANY PRIOR **POLITICAL OR MILITARY EXPERIENCE.**

In a shocking upset, Donald Trump beat his rival, Hillary Clinton, on November 8, 2016, despite losing the popular vote. This has only happened four other times in American election history! Stocks and foreign markets plunged overnight as the world panicked at the news of the businessman's rise to leader of the free world. By the morning, however, things started to settle down.

Trump has promised many things to the American people, including his number one campaign promise: to "Make America Great Again."

WALLED UP

Before the election, many became wary of Trump's America, since many of his campaign promises also seemed to take away some hard-won liberties. Trump promised to reverse Obamacare, build a wall along the Mexican border, deport illegal immigrants, refuse entry to refugees from "terror-prone regions," temporarily ban any foreign Muslims from the country, "bomb" ISIS, reverse women's reproductive rights and gay marriage rights, repeal climate change programs, create jobs by ending a trade agreement signed by President Clinton (NAFTA), and lower taxes, among other things.

ELECTION SELECTION

Experts say that some voters in America felt like they weren't being heard by "elites" in Washington. Poll numbers showed that 7 out of 10 Americans didn't like the direction the country was going. So these voters went to the polls, and in the winner-take-all electoral college, Trump won the country. He has a lot of work cut out for him after a vicious election season, so he began his acceptance speech with a humble tone of hope. What will his legacy be? Only time will tell!

and decided to stay on as an executive producer of his reality TV show *The Celebrity Apprentice*.

WHY HE'S WEIRD!

DONALD TRUMP IS A BUSINESSMAN, AND THAT MEANS HE KNOWS MONEY. AFTER RECEIVING A $14 MILLION LOAN FROM HIS FATHER, TRUMP WON (AND LOST) MILLIONS OF HIS OWN DOLLARS IN REAL ESTATE AND CASINO BUSINESS VENTURES. WITH HIS FORTUNE AND FAME, DONALD TRUMP HAS PUT HIS NAME ON HUGE, SKY-SCRAPING TOWERS, BOUGHT A BEAUTY PAGEANT, CREATED HIS OWN REALITY TELEVISION SHOW, AND RUN FOR PRESIDENT OF THE UNITED STATES.

LIFE AFTER

It takes a lot of ambition and maybe a little bit of craziness to want to be president of the United States. And assuming the highest office in the land isn't without its risks. After all that adventure, it'd be hard to blame them for wanting to relax. But not all presidents did. Some took to retirement a bit more energetically than others.

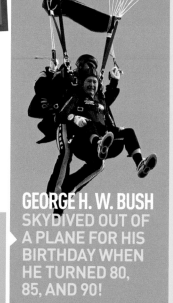

GEORGE H. W. BUSH SKYDIVED OUT OF A PLANE FOR HIS BIRTHDAY WHEN HE TURNED 80, 85, AND 90!

JIMMY CARTER won the Nobel Peace Prize "for his decades of untiring effort to find peaceful solutions to international conflicts."

ULYSSES S. GRANT HURRIEDLY WROTE HIS MEMOIRS FOR MARK TWAIN TO PUBLISH AS HE WAS DYING—AND FINISHED THEM FIVE DAYS BEFORE HIS DEATH. THEY'RE CONSIDERED AMONG THE BEST PRESIDENTIAL AUTOBIOGRAPHIES.

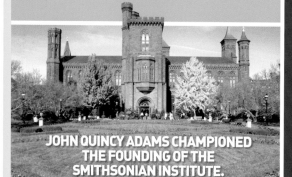

JOHN QUINCY ADAMS CHAMPIONED THE FOUNDING OF THE SMITHSONIAN INSTITUTE.

TEDDY ROOSEVELT explored the River of Doubt, a previously unknown tributary of the Amazon River.

GEORGE W. BUSH painted pictures of puppies and people, (and two of him taking a bath!). His paintings have even been in museums and discussed by art critics!

WILLIAM TAFT SERVED ON THE SUPREME COURT AS CHIEF JUSTICE.

BILL CLINTON CURBED HIS JUNK-FOOD-JUNKIE HABITS AND BECAME AN ADVOCATE FOR HEALTHIER EATING AFTER NEEDING HEART BYPASS SURGERY.

STUMP YOUR PARENTS

PRESIDENTIAL POP QUIZ

See if your parents are up to speed by quizzing their knowledge on all things presidential.

(ANSWERS BELOW)

1 Which president dedicated the Statue of Liberty?
a. Rutherford B. Hayes
b. Grover Cleveland
c. George Washington
d. Theodore Roosevelt

2 What did James Madison not help write?
a. The Federalist Papers
b. The Constitution
c. The Declaration of Independence
d. The Bill of Rights

3 How many presidents have been impeached (and acquitted)?
a. 1
b. 2
c. 3
d. 10

4 Which president's kids took their pony on the White House elevator?
a. James K. Polk
b. Barack Obama
c. Harry S. Truman
d. Theodore Roosevelt

5 Who was the only president to start his professional career as a model?
a. Gerald Ford
b. Donald J. Trump
c. Ronald Reagan
d. Barack Obama

6 Which president grew up speaking Dutch?
a. Martin Van Buren
b. William Henry Harrison
c. Barack Obama
d. Herbert Hoover

ANSWERS: 1.b; 2.c; 3.b; 4.d; 5.a; 6.a

GREAT MINDS THINK ALIKE

Have you ever heard the phrase "Great minds think alike"? Well, the U.S. presidents had more in common than just being president. Check out these surprising (and sometimes bizarre) things they had in common!

★ ★ ★ ★ ★

FIVE-STAR GENERALS

Ulysses S. Grant and
Dwight D. Eisenhower

★ ★ ★ ★ ★

NARROWLY AVOIDED DEATH IN WWII
John F. Kennedy, Lyndon B. Johnson,
Gerald Ford, and George H. W. Bush

DONATED PRESIDENTIAL SALARY TO CHARITY
Herbert Hoover and JFK

DIED ON THE SAME DAY
Thomas Jefferson and John Adams
(**July 4, 1826,** exactly 50 years from the day they
both signed the Declaration of Independence)

Became a FAMOUS LAWYER WITHOUT GOING TO LAW SCHOOL

John Quincy Adams and Abraham Lincoln

HELD ICE-CREAM JOBS

Dwight D. Eisenhower and Barack Obama

INDENTURED SERVANTS

Millard Fillmore and Andrew Johnson

HAD A QUAKER UPBRINGING
Herbert Hoover and Richard Nixon

WERE CHEERLEADERS
FDR, Dwight D. Eisenhower, Ronald Reagan, and George W. Bush

MOST PECULIAR PRESIDENTS

① GEORGE WASHINGTON

Back in Washington's day, it was sometimes hard to tell if a person was really dead or just a deep sleeper. Washington was so worried about being buried alive, that he insisted mourners wait at least three days before burying him. Just in case.

② ANDREW JACKSON

Jackson loved a good duel. In his most memorable, his opponent, Charles Dickinson, fired off a shot, hitting Jackson square in the chest. That stung, but Jackson carefully took aim and killed Dickinson. Jackson carried the bullet close to his heart for the rest of his life.

③ ABRAHAM LINCOLN

Abraham Lincoln hated being called Abe so much, even his wife called him Mr. Lincoln!

④ THEODORE ROOSEVELT

Move over, Batman, Teddy Roosevelt's in Gotham. As New York City police commissioner, Teddy took his job extremely seriously. He'd go 40 hours without sleeping in order to patrol neighborhoods. He was reforming the corrupt police system, and making sure policemen weren't dozing on the job. He even had a special outfit tailored for his "midnight rambles": a black cape, cane, and hat.

⑤ WOODROW WILSON

When Wilson was recovering from a stroke, he liked to take in the scenery in Washington, D.C. What he didn't like was other drivers going faster than him. It was only the persistence of his drivers that talked him out of arresting speed demons going faster than his preferred pace of 10 miles an hour (16 km/h).

slow down

⑥ JIMMY CARTER

Jimmy is the only president to have reported seeing a UFO. Some astronomers claim he really saw the planet Venus, but Jimmy stuck to his story.

⑦ CALVIN COOLIDGE

Besides luxuriating in Vaseline head rubs and taking hours-long naps in the afternoon after a nine-hour good night's sleep, Coolidge spent a weird amount of time with curtains. He'd dreamily tie the cords into knots and hide from the White House staff in them!

⑧ RONALD REAGAN

Ronald Reagan had a bad habit. He smoked. In order to help quit, he started eating jelly beans instead. Jelly Belly was his go-to bean brand, and they supplied the president with the goods for all eight years of his presidency. His favorite flavor was licorice.

⑨ BILL CLINTON

To emulate a favorite professor in college, Clinton started eating entire apples—core, seeds, and stem included. His professor insisted the minerals were in the core.

⑩ BARACK OBAMA

Ice cream may be America's frozen treat of choice in the summer, but Obama hates the sweet stuff! He says it's thanks to his teenage job at Baskin-Robbins.

WHICH IS WEIRDER?

	OR	
HAVING A RUBBER JAW (GROVER CLEVELAND)	OR	HAVING DENTURES MADE IN PART FROM IVORY FROM HIPPOS (GEORGE WASHINGTON)
GIVING YOUR DOG A SEAT AT CABINET MEETINGS (WARREN HARDING)	OR	KEEPING YOUR PET ALLIGATOR IN THE WHITE HOUSE BATHTUB (JOHN QUINCY ADAMS)
TRACKING, KILLING, AND STUFFING YOUR OWN PREY (TEDDY ROOSEVELT)	OR	PARDONING A PET TURKEY (ABRAHAM LINCOLN)
EATING COTTAGE CHEESE WITH KETCHUP (RICHARD NIXON)	OR	EATING AN OPOSSUM (WILLIAM TAFT)

what?!

PRESIDENTS' PRANKS

DON'T TRY THIS AT HOME!

ANDREW JACKSON
dug up other people's OUTHOUSES in the middle of the night.

ABRAHAM LINCOLN
TOLD A BUNCH OF BOYS PLAYING CATCH WITH A **PIG'S BLADDER** (THE 1800s VERSION OF A BALLOON) THAT IT WOULD BE FUNNIER IF THEY THREW IT IN THE FIRE AND HEATED IT UP FIRST. THEY DID. IT **EXPLODED** AND HE LAUGHED.

GERALD FORD
LIKED TO BLAME HIS SECRET SERVICE MEN WHEN HE **PASSED GAS,** SAYING, "WAS THAT YOU? SHOW SOME CLASS!"

Lyndon B. Johnson
invited friends for a joyride in his new car, then PRETENDED the brakes were out while racing down a hill toward a lake. While everyone else SCREAMED, he LAUGHED hysterically, letting his car slide into the lake.

{ IT WAS AN AMPHICAR—A CAR FOR HIGHWAYS AND WATERWAYS. }

GROVER CLEVELAND
pulled gates off fences, snuck into the town's bell tower, and rang it late at night to **WAKE PEOPLE UP.**

JOHN TYLER LOCKED HIS TEACHER IN A CLOSET FOR BEING TOO STRICT.

GEORGE W. BUSH WAS ALWAYS REMEMBERED AS THE CLASS CLOWN WILLING TO DO ANYTHING FOR A LAUGH—EVEN **DRAWING ON HIS FACE** TO MIMIC ELVIS.

JIMMY CARTER CONVINCED HIS SISTER TO BURY A NICKEL TO GROW A NICKEL TREE, **THEN DUG UP THE NICKEL WHEN SHE LEFT.**

CALVIN COOLIDGE USED TO PRESS ALL THE BUTTONS ON HIS DESK AND HIDE WHILE HIS STAFF WENT RUNNING AROUND THE WHITE HOUSE LOOKING FOR HIM!

FRANKLIN D. ROOSEVELT PUT EFFERVESCING POWDER IN HIS NURSE'S CHAMBER POT, SO WHEN SHE WENT TO THE BATHROOM IN THE MIDDLE OF THE NIGHT, IT BUBBLED UP, MAKING HER THINK SOMETHING WAS SERIOUSLY WRONG WITH HER HEALTH.

John F. Kennedy changed a restaurant sign from "NO DOGS" to "NO HOT DOGS."

HE LOVED PRANKS SO MUCH, HE FORMED A CLUB CALLED THE MUCKERS. ITS MEMBERS LIKED TO MUCK STUFF UP.

INDEX

INDEX

INDEX

PHOTO CREDITS

FRONT COVER: (LO LE), Adrian Lubbers; (LO CTR), Digital Media Pro/SS; **SPINE:** (UP), Adrian Lubbers; (CTR), Digital Media Pro/SS; **BACK COVER:** (UP LE), Adrian Lubbers; (CTR RT), Richard Peterson/SS; (LO), Comstock

Illustrations throughout by Adrian Lubbers.

Abbreviations: GI=Getty Images; LC=Library of Congress Prints and Photographs Division; SS=Shutterstock

1 (UP), Wes Abrams/GI; 2-3, Photodisc; 4-5 (UP), Comstock; 4 (UP LE), Eric Thayer/Reuters/Newscom; 4 (UP CTR), cynoclub/SS; 4 (UP RT), Heritage Auctions, Dallas; 4 (LO LE), BrandX/NGS; 4 (LO CTR), Heritage Auctions, Dallas; 4 (LO LE), Cris Stoddard/GI; 5 (UP CTR), Heritage Auctions, Dallas; 5 (UP RT), Heritage Auctions, Dallas; 5 (LO LE), Sean Pavone/SS; 6-7, S.Borisov/SS; 8 (6 frame), Kamil Macniak/SS; 8 (UP LE), Stephen Mcsweeny/SS; 9 (UP), Brandon Bourdages/SS; 9 (LO RT), Stock-Asso/SS; 10 (UP), White House Historical Association; 10 (LO), Image Catcher News Service/GI; 11, Vadim Sadovski/SS; 13, Wlad74/SS; 14 (UP LE), VitoriusT/SS; 14 (CTR), Granger.com—All rights reserved; 14 (CTR RT), Stock Montage/GI; 15 (UP RT), Universal History Archive/GI; 16 (UP LE), AISA/Everett Collection, Inc.; 16 (UP CTR), Superstock/Everett Collection, Inc.; 17 (LO), Yale University Art Gallery, New Haven/Bridgeman Images; 18 (INSET), Granger.com—All rights reserved; 19 (UP), US Capitol Collection, Washington D.C./Boltin Picture Library/Bridgeman Images; 19 (LO), Massachusetts Historical Society/Bridgeman Images; 20, White House Historical Association; 21, Natalia Barsukova/SS; 23, LC; 23 (LO CTR), Lev Kropotov/SS; 24, The U.S. National Archives and Records Administration; 25 (UP), Granger.com—All rights reserved; 25 (UP CTR), Vitaly Korovin/SS; 25 (CTR RT), Everett—Art/SS; 26, David David Gallery, Philadelphia/Bridgeman Images; 27 (UP), haveseen/SS; 27 (LO), Sarin Images/Granger.com—All rights reserved; 29 (UP), ID1974/SS; 29 (LO), Granger.com—All rights reserved; 30 (CTR), Stephen Rees/SS; 30 (LO), North Wind Picture Archives/Alamy Stock Photo; 31 (CTR LE), Wally Stemberger/SS; 31 (UP RT), Lucie Lang/SS; 31 (LO RT), Everett Historical/SS; 33 (CTR RT), Hemera Technologies/GI; 33 (LO RT), Granger.com—All rights reserved; 34 (UP), Jo Crebbin/SS; 34 (UP CTR), Callahan/SS; 34 (LO LE), Robert Gebbie Photography/SS; 35 (UP RT), C Squared Studios/GI; 35 (CTR), LC; 35 (LO), Malyugin/SS; 37 (UP RT), Eric Isselee/SS; 37 (LO RT), Kitch Bain/SS; 37 (LO LE), MrPhotoMania/SS; 38 (CTR LE), ullstein bild/GI; 38 (LO), Cincinnati Observatory; 39 (UP RT), Sihasakprachum/SS; 39 (CTR RT), Dolly MJ/SS; 39 (LO), United States Mint; 41 (CTR LE), Lisa S./SS; 41 (CTR RT), Granger.com—All rights reserved; 41 (LO CTR), Tim UR/SS; 42-43 (UP), Granger.com—All rights reserved; 42 (LO), cynoclub/SS; 43 (LO), Granger.com—All rights reserved; 44 (UP), George D Lepp/GI; 44 (LO), Illinskiy Anatoliy/SS; 45 (UP), Maks Narodenko/SS; 45 (LO), Everett Collection Historical/Alamy Stock Photo; 46 (CTR), Aleksandrs Bondars/SS; 46 (LO LE), Anan Kaewkhammul/SS; 47 (UP), Kevin George/SS; 47 (LO), Anan Kaewkhammul/SS; 49 (UP RT), Mega Pixel/SS; 49 (CTR LE), Heritage Auctions, Dallas; 49 (LO RT), Heritage Auctions, Dallas; 51 (UP), Gladskikh Tatiana/SS; 51 (LO RT), Historic Map Works LLC and Osher Map Library/GI; 51 (LO LE), windu/SS; 53 (UP), Brian A Jackson/SS; 53 (LO RT), Susan H. Douglas Political Americana Collection #2214/Cornell University Library, Rare & Manuscript Collections; 54 (UP), LC; 54 (LO), Sarin Images/Granger.com—All rights reserved; 55 (LO), LC; 56 (UP LE), Preto Perola/SS; 56 (LO LE), mashuk/SS; 56 (LO RT), Nattika/SS; 57 (LO LE), Granger.com—All rights reserved; 57 (LO RT), akiyoko/SS; 58 (UP), North Wind Picture Archives/Alamy Stock Photo; 58 (LO LE), LC; 59 (dog), cynoclub/GI; 59 (cup), Debu55y/SS; 60 (UP), Granger.com—All rights reserved; 60 (CTR RT), Universal Images Group/GI; 60 (LO LE), andersphoto/SS; 61 (LO LE), Sarin Images/Granger.com—All rights reserved; 62 (UP), Granger.com—All rights reserved; 62 (CTR LE), Granger.com—All rights reserved; 62 (LO LE), Corbis/VCG via GI; 63 (UP CTR RT), LC; 63 (LO CTR RT), wayarch/SS; 63 (LO LE), LC; 65 (CAT), Elena Rudyk/SS; 65 (PLATE), urfin/SS; 65 (CTR RT), Hulton Archive/GI; 65 (LO RT), Dutch Scenery/GI; 66 (UP), LC; 67 (LO), LC; 67 (UP), LC; 67 (UP CTR RT), Heritage Auctions, Dallas; 67 (LO CTR RT), Kean Collection/GI; 67 (LO RT), LC; 68 (CTR LE), LC; 69, Photography by Dmitry Chernomazov; 71 (CTR), cosma/SS; 71 (LO), Sarin Images/Granger.com—All rights reserved; 72 (CTR LE), LC; 73 (UP), LC; 73 (LO), Granger.com—All rights reserved; 75 (UP), Eric Isselee/SS; 75 (CTR), LC; 75 (LO), Heritage Auctions, Dallas; 76 (UP), LC; 76 (LO RT), Olga Popova/SS; 77, LC; 78 (LO), Africa Studio/SS; 79 (CTR), Tiplyashina Evgeniya/SS; 81 (UP), S1001/SS; 81 (CTR), Granger.com—All rights reserved; 81 (LO), The Image Bank/GI; 83 (UP), Leena Robinson/SS; 83 (hat), Wes Abrams/GI; 83 (LO RT), LC; 89 (LO RT), sign), dennizn/SS; 83 (clothes), Syda Productions/SS; 85, LC; 87 (CTR LE), Jeff Mauritzen/National Geographic Creative; 87 (LO LE), Twixx/Dreamstime; 87 (LO CTR), Vereshchagin Dmitry/SS; 87 (LO RT), Filmwork_52/Dreamstime; 89 (UP), Dudarev Mikhail/SS; 89 (LO RT), LC; 89 (LO LE), Hulton Archive/GI; 90 (UP RT), Sarita Sutthisakari/SS; 90-91 (CTR), CoraMax/SS; 90 (LO LE), GlobalP/GI; 91 (LO RT), World History Archive/Alamy Stock Photo; 91 (CTR RT), jaroslava V/SS; 93 (UP), Photodisc; 93 (LO), LC; 94 (UP LE), LC; 94 (LO RT), Nattika/SS; 94 (LO RT), Molnar Jozsef/SS; 95 (CTR), Evgeniya Uvarova/SS; 95 (LO RT), Watch_The_World/SS; 96 (UP), Kruglov_Orda/SS; 96 (lion), Eric Isselee/SS; 96 (cat), Johanna Goodyear/Dreamstime; 96 (bear), Eric Isselee/SS; 96 (LO RT), Lynn Y/SS; 97, Jody Dingle/Dreamstime; 98 (LO RT), Bryan Solomon/SS; 99 (CTR RT), Anderson Americana; 99 (LO LE), White House Historical Association; 101 (UP RT), grynold/SS; 101 (LO RT), LC; 102 (UP LE), Education Images/GI; 102 (CTR RT), elnavegante/SS; 102 (LO LE), Pictorial Press Ltd/Alamy Stock Photo; 103 (UP RT), Gayvoronskaya_Yana/SS; 103 (LO), Photos.com/GI; 104 (UP LE), LC; 104 (LO RT), AFP/GI; 105 (LO), Dmitry Abaza/SS; 106 (LO LE), LC; 106 (LO CTR), LC; 107 (LO RT), Swapan Photography/SS; 107 (LO RT), PhotoQuest/GI; 108 (UP), Hurst Photo/SS; 108 (LO), Granger.com—All rights reserved; 109 (chicken), Steshkin Yevgeniy/SS; 109 (pot), Evgeny Karandaev/SS; 109 (LO LE), PhotoQuest/GI; 109 (CTR), spaxiax/SS; 110 (UP LE), Matej Hudovernik/SS; 110 (LO LE), Serhiy Shullye/SS; 111 (LE), olavs/SS; 111 (LO), Everett Historical/SS; 112 (LE), National Archives & Records Administration—Hoover Presidential Library; 112 (RT), LC; 113 (LO RT), Hulton Archive/GI; 114 (CTR LE), catwalker/SS; 114 (CTR), catwalker/SS; 114 (LO LE), Thomas D. McAvoy/GI; 114 (LO RT), Roma74/Dreamstime; 115, Universal History Archive/GI; 116 (UP), Everett Historical/SS; 116 (CTR), Kaesler Media/SS; 116 (LO), Everett Historical/SS; 117, National Archives; 118 (UP), IWM/GI; 118 (LO RT), LC; 120 (UP), LanKS/SS; 121 (chart), Photodisc; 121 (bat), Boonchuay Promjiam/SS; 121 (CTR LE), cubart/SS; 121 (LO), Popperfoto/GI; 122 (UP), CBS Photo Archive/GI; 122 (TV), Gino Santa Maria/SS; 122 (LO RT), George Skadding/GI; 123 (LO RT), Dwight D. Eisenhower Library and Museum; 124 (UP LE), aboutsung/SS; 124 (LO), Adam Glickman/Underwood Archives/GI; 125 (UP RT), Bettmann/GI; 125 (CTR RT), stockernumber2/SS; 125 (LO), Bettmann/GI; 126 (CTR LE), Bettmann/GI; 126 (LO CTR), Alexanderphoto7/SS; 127 (LO RT), Lemusique/SS; 128 (UP RT), Bettmann/GI; 128 (LO RT), Rosemary Harris/Alamy Stock Photo; 128 (LO CTR), Bettmann/GI; 128 (LO RT), NotarYES/SS; 129, NASA; 130 (UP RT), LC; 130 (CTR RT), 360b/SS; 130 (CTR LE), Rod Collins/Alamy Stock Photo; 131 (LO), Javier Brosch/SS; 132 (UP LE), LBJ Library photo by Cecil Stoughton; 132 (LO CTR), Steven Cukrov/Dreamstime; 132 (LO RT), terekhov igor/SS; 133 (UP), LBJ Library photo by Cecil Stoughton; 133 (LO), Bettmann/GI; 134 (UP), Jill Freedman/GI; 134 (LO), Brian A Jackson/SS; 135 (CTR LE), luca85/SS; 135 (LO), Warongdech/SS; 136 (UP), Bettmann/GI; 136 (CTR RT), Hulton Archive/GI; 137 (CTR LE), MCT/GI; 137 (LO RT), Bettmann/GI; 138 (UP), Keystone Pictures USA/Alamy Stock Photo; 138 (INSET), Claudio Divizia/SS; 138 (LO RT), Iasha/SS; 139 (CTR LE), Viktorus/SS; 139 (LO), Bettmann/GI; 140 (UP), Bill Pierce/GI; 140 (LO), Bettmann/GI; 141 (LO), Courtesy Hearst; 142 (UP LE), Courtesy Gerald R. Ford Library; 142 (UP RT), Peter Keegan/GI; 142 (CTR RT), bendao/SS; 142 (LO LE), White House Photograph Courtesy Gerald R. Ford Library; 143 (LO), Hong Vo/SS; 144 (UP RT), Owen Franken/GI; 144 (UP CTR), Lim Yong Hian/SS; 144 (CTR RT), AP Photo/Harvey Georges; 144 (LO LE), Ingrid Prats/Dreamstime; 145 (UP RT), AP Photo; 145 (CTR LE), De Agostini/A. Dagli Orti/GI; 145 (LO), David Hume Kennerly/GI; 146 (CTR LE), New York Daily News/GI; 146 (LO), Bettmann/GI; 147 (CTR LE), damedeeso/GI; 147 (LO RT), Corbis Historical/GI; 148 (UP LE), Heritage Auctions, Dallas; 148 (LO RT), Warner Bros/REX/SS; 149 (UP LE), Gorobets/SS; 149 (UP RT), Mike Sargent/AFP/GI; 149 (CTR RT), Bildagentur Zoonar GmbH/SS; 149 (LO), ullstein bild/GI; 150 (UP LE), Photodisc; 150 (CTR RT), Franck Boston/SS; 151 (CTR LE), Notto Yeez/SS; 151 (LO LE), xavier gallego morell/SS; 151 (LO RT), Carol T. Powers/GI; 152 (UP), Catherine Henriette/GI; 152 (LO RT), Gerard Malie/AFP/GI; 152 (LO LE), Lisa Mckown/Dreamstime; 152 (CTR LE), Consolidated News Pictures/GI; 153 (CTR RT), Terrace Studio/SS; 153 (LO), Charles Caratini/GI; 154 (UP), Artville; 155 (CTR RT), Stuart Monk/SS; 155 (LO), J David Ake/AFP/GI; 156 (UP LE), Rolls Press/Popperfoto/GI; 156 (CTR RT), Trinacria Photo/SS; 156 (CTR), Tatiana Popova/SS; 157 (UP), Michael Reynolds/EPA/Alamy Stock Photo; 157 (LO), YamabikaY/SS; 158 (UP RT), TIM CLARY/AFP/GI; 158 (LO), AP Photo/Hansi Krauss; 159 (UP RT), William J. Clinton Presidential Library; 159 (CTR LE), railway fx/SS; 159 (LO CTR RT), New York Daily News Archive/GI; 159 (LO RT), AP Photo/Ed Betz; 160 (LO LE), Kletr/SS; 161 (UP RT), Couperfield/SS; 161 (CTR LE), Staff/Reuters; 161 (LO RT), Evikka/SS; 162, Robert Giroux/GI; 163 (UP LE), Chip Somodevilla/GI; 163 (CTR RT), Scanrail1/SS; 164, Win McNamee/GI; 165 (UP LE), Nick Starichenko/SS; 165 (UP LE), Ranjith Ravindran/SS; 165 (CTR RT), AP Photo/APTN; 165 (CTR RT), AP Photo/APTN; 165 (CTR RT), AP Photo/APTN; 167 (UP), Justin Sullivan/GI; 167 (LO RT), White House Photo/Alamy Stock Photo; 167 (LO LE), artjazz/SS; 168 (UP), Rick Friedman/GI; 168 (LO), Courtesy of Marvel; 169 (UP RT), 5 Second Studio/SS; 169 (CTR RT), Theresa Martinez/SS; 169 (LO), epa european pressphoto agency b.v./Alamy Stock Photo; 170 (CTR LE), Official White House Photo by Chuck Kennedy; 170 (LO LE), Africa Studio/SS; 171 (UP), Thomas A. Ferrara-Pool/GI; 173, Mike Segar/Reuters; 174 (UP RT), AP Photo/College Station Eagle, Gabriel Chmielewski; 174 (LO CTR RT), George Rinhart/GI; 174 (LO RT), ifong/SS; 174 (LO LE), AP Photo/Benny Snyder; 174 (CTR LE), Vanessagifford/Dreamstime; 175 (UP), Steve Collender/SS; 175 (CTR LE), LC; 175 (LO RT), luismonteiro/SS; 176 (UP LE), Misti Dawson/EyeEm/GI; 176 (CTR RT), Kokhanchikov/SS; 176 (Adams), Granger.com—All rights reserved; 176 (marker), Mkopka/Dreamstime; 176 (Jefferson), Superstock/Everett Collection, Inc.; 177 (UP CTR), Rafa Irusta/SS; 177 (CTR RT), gresei/SS; 177 (LO), Darren McCollester/GI; 177 (CTR LE), cosma/SS; 178 (UP RT), North Wind Picture Archives/Alamy Stock Photo; 178 (CTR LE), MPI/GI; 178 (LO RT), LC; 179 (UP RT), Mega Pixel/SS; 179 (UP CTR RT), RoJo Images/SS; 179 (LO RT), Tony Wear/SS; 179 (LO LE), Dmitry Kalinovsky/SS; 179 (CTR LE), photopeerayut/SS; 182-183 (UP), Comstock; 183 (LO LE), cynoclub/SS; 184-185 (UP), Comstock; 186-187 (UP), Comstock; 187 (LO LE), BrandX/NGS; 188-189 (UP), Comstock; 191, Digital Media Pro/SS

CREDITS

For Tim, my partner in all things —B.D.

Since 1888, the National Geographic Society has funded more than 14,000 research, conservation, education, and storytelling projects around the world. National Geographic Partners distributes a portion of the funds it receives from your purchase to National Geographic Society to support programs including the conservation of animals and their habitats. To learn more, visit natgeo.com/info.

For more information, visit nationalgeographic.com, call 1-877-873-6846, or write to the following address:

National Geographic Partners, LLC
1145 17th Street N.W.
Washington, DC 20036-4688 U.S.A.

For librarians and teachers: nationalgeographic.com/books/librarians-and-educators

More for kids from National Geographic: natgeokids.com

National Geographic Kids magazine inspires children to explore their world with fun yet educational articles on animals, science, nature, and more. Using fresh storytelling and amazing photography, *Nat Geo Kids* shows kids ages 6 to 14 the fascinating truth about the world—and why they should care. **natgeo.com/subscribe**

For rights or permissions inquiries, please contact National Geographic Books Subsidiary Rights: bookrights@natgeo.com

Designed by Rachael Hamm Plett, Moduza Design

Library of Congress Cataloging-in-Publication Data
Names: National Geographic Society (U.S.)
Title: U.S. presidents.
Other titles: US presidents.
Description: Washington, DC : National Geographic, 2017. | Series: Weird but true know-it-all | Audience: Grades 4 to 6. | Includes index.
Identifiers: LCCN 2016051360| ISBN 9781426327971 (hardcover : alkaline paper) | ISBN 9781426327964 (paperback : alkaline paper)
Subjects: LCSH: Presidents--United States--Biography--Miscellanea--Juvenile literature. | Curiosities and wonders--United States--Juvenile literature.| BISAC: JUVENILE NONFICTION/History/United States/General.
Classification: LCC E176.1 .U155 2017 | DDC 973.09/9--dc23
LC record available at https://lccn.loc.gov/2016051360

The publisher would like to thank everyone who helped make this book possible: Ariane Szu-Tu, associate editor; Becky Baines, executive editor; Sarah J. Mock, senior photo editor; Alix Inchausti, production editor; and Gus Tello and Anne LeongSon, production designers. And a special thank-you to Robert D. Johnston, associate professor and director of the Teaching of History program at the University of Illinois at Chicago, and fact-checkers Greg Geddes, Scott Vehstedt, and James D. Jeffery for their expert reviews.

Printed in Canada
21/FC/4 (PB)
21/FC/2 (RLB)

IF YOU ENJOYED THESE WACKY FACTS

about our country's presidents, there's so much more to explore in this amazing encyclopedia of our leaders, from Washington to Trump.

Official portraits • Quotes Stories • Speeches • Stats Pets • More cool stuff

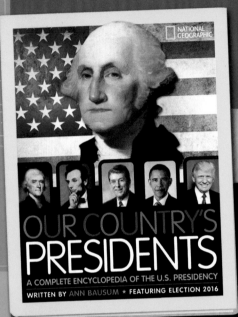